KU-795-855

Handbook of
Patient-Controlled Analgesia

Dilip V. Subhedar, M.D.
*Associate Chief of Service, Metropolitan Hospital,
New York; Assistant Professor of Anesthesiology,
New York Medical College, Valhalla*

Vinod Malik, M.D.
*Instructor in Anesthesiology, New York Medical College,
Valhalla; Director of Pain Services, Department of
Anesthesiology, Lincoln Medical and Mental Health
Center, Bronx, New York*

Dariusz Rudz, M.D.
*Assistant Professor of Anesthesiology, New York Medical
College, Valhalla; Attending Anesthesiologist, Lincoln
Medical and Mental Health Center, Bronx, New York*

Foreword by Elizabeth A.M. Frost, M.D.
*Professor and Chair, Department of Anesthesiology,
New York Medical College, Valhalla*

Butterworth–Heinemann

Boston   Oxford   Johannesburg   Melbourne   New Delhi   Singapore

Every effort has been made to ensure that the drug dosage schedules within this text are accurate and conform to standards accepted at time of publication. However, as treatment recommendations vary in the light of continuing research and clinical experience, the reader is advised to verify drug dosage schedules herein with information found on product information sheets. This is especially true in cases of new or infrequently used drugs.

∞ Recognizing the importance of preserving what has been written, Butterworth–Heinemann prints its books on acid-free paper whenever possible.

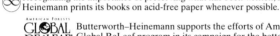

AMERICAN FORESTS
GLOBAL
ReLeaf
2000
Butterworth–Heinemann supports the efforts of American Forests and the Global ReLeaf program in its campaign for the betterment of trees, forests, and our environment.

Library of Congress Cataloging-in-Publication Data

Subhedar, Dilip V.
    Handbook of patient-controlled analgesia / Dilip V. Subhedar,
Vinod Malik, Dariusz Rudz ; foreword by Elizabeth A.M. Frost.
        p. cm.
    Includes bibliographical references and index.
    ISBN 0-7506-9865-9 (alk. paper)
    1. Patient-controlled analgesia--Handbooks, manuals, etc.
I. Malik, Vinod. II. Rudz, Dariusz. III. Title.
    [DNLM: 1. Analgesia, Patient-Controlled--handbooks. 2. Pain--drug
therapy--handbooks.   WO 39 S941h 1997]
RD98.4.S83 1997
615'.783--dc21
DNLM/DLC
for Library of Congress   97-16057
                                                                      CIP

British Library Cataloguing-in-Publication Data
A catalogue record for this book is available from the British Library.

The publisher offers special discounts on bulk orders of this book.
For information, please contact:

Manager of Special Sales
Butterworth–Heinemann
313 Washington Street
Newton, MA 02158-1626
Tel: 617-928-2500
Fax: 617-928-2620

For information on all
Butterworth–Heinemann publications
available, contact our World Wide Web
home page at: http://www.bh.com

10 9 8 7 6 5 4 3 2 1

Printed in the United States of America.

*To our families, who watched us put in hours of
preparation for this book that could have
been time spent with them.*

*To our chair, Elizabeth A.M. Frost, who has inspired,
supported, and helped us to complete this book.*

*To our readers who may use the material
to improve patient care.*

Contents

Foreword

For all the happiness mankind can gain
is not in pleasure, but in rest from pain.
————John Dryden, *The Indian Emperor*, 1665

Pleasure is nothing else but the intermission of pain.
————John Seldon, *Table Talk (Pleasure)*, 1689

Absolute morality is the regulation of conduct in
such a way that pain shall not be inflicted.
————Herbert Spencer, *Essays, Vol. 3: Prison Echoes*, 1891

There was a faith healer of Deal
Who said "Although pain isn't real,
If I sit on a pin
And it punctures my skin,
I dislike what I fancy I feel."
————Anonymous, *Week-End Book*, 1925

These four quotations speak volumes about our perceptions of pain.
Many practitioners, whether voluntarily or involuntarily, still consider
pain the affliction of a weak mind. They believe, perhaps subcon-
sciously, that those who complain of pain have reduced tolerance or
must be products of a lesser culture. Nevertheless, as is emphasized in
the old English rhyming couplet, a surgical wound hurts. Hippocrates
advised all physicians to do no harm. Centuries later, an English
philosopher linked morality to a conduct that disallowed pain. But

the most poignant utterances relate to the peace that comes from the ending of pain.

The concept of self-administration of intravenous analgesics was developed at least 30 years ago. It is remarkable that even today the idea has not gained universal acceptance, sometimes I suspect, for reasons that do not confirm the supposed altruism of the medical profession. Recently, I was face to face with an all-too-common situation. My mother fell and broke her scapula. She was admitted to a geriatric hospital in the United Kingdom complaining of considerable pain, which persisted for weeks. Her medical attendants assured me that they were satisfied with the every-6-hours narcotic medication she was receiving. I inquired as to the possibility of using a patient-controlled analgesia system. The suggestion was rejected: She was considered to be too old at 89 years, the technique was unsuitable for a ward setting, and, moreover, it would require an anesthetic consultation.

I believe that the same kind of situation may also occur in the United States. In this text, three anesthesiologists have set out to dispel much of the mystique of patient-controlled analgesia. I applaud their presention of the technique as simple, effective, and inexpensive and one that should and can be adopted worldwide—not just in the perioperative environment but also in outpatient settings, cancer facilities, and even the home. Perhaps the time is approaching when we will come a bit closer to the perfect state described in the Book of Revelation: "And God shall wipe away all tears from their eyes—neither shall there be any more pain."

ELIZABETH A.M. FROST

Preface

Studies suggest that at many centers, pain is undertreated despite the advances made in the field of pain medicine, in both drugs and delivery systems. Patient-controlled analgesia (PCA) is one such modality that is well accepted by patients when properly introduced. Despite the potential of PCA to provide superior analgesia, haphazard and disorganized implementation programs may doom the technique to sporadic use and eventual abandonment.

PCA is not a new development in the field of pain management. Yet this safe, easy, and effective modality remains underused. Part of the problem involves reimbursement issues and hospital policies. Equally true, however, is the fact that several types of practitioners (e.g., surgical residents, anesthesia residents, nurses, and emergency room personnel) often do not understand the hardware and relevant opioid pharmacology and pharmacokinetics and thus neglect to incorporate PCA into their practice.

This handbook brings together the essential information required for bedside use of PCA, including information on PCA systems, opioid pharmacology and dosages, and recommendations for its use in various disease states. Recommendations for monitoring and treating untoward effects are outlined. It is not the purpose of this handbook to provide a detailed examination of neurophysiology, pain transmission, or any such information not directly related to the practical use of PCA.

Throughout the book, we have included tables and easy-to-understand figures. Complex graphs and scientific studies have been excluded, in keeping with our concept of the book as a primer and ready reference for PCA use throughout the hospital. Discussions of the newer modalities of PCA—that is, patient-controlled epidural analgesia and patient-controlled subcutaneous analgesia—are included.

Although pain control is the domain of anesthesiologists, this book will probably be used by residents in surgery, anesthesiology, obstetrics, and emergency medicine; nurses on the wards and in post-operative care units; and practitioners interested in starting a PCA service in their hospitals.

DVS
VM
DR

1

Introduction to Patient-Controlled Analgesia

Patient-controlled analgesia (PCA), or demand analgesia, is a widespread and well-accepted method of modern pain management. PCA enables patients to self-administer a prescribed dose of an analgesic at their earliest perception of pain. It also enables patients to control the amount and timing of analgesia they receive. Although the majority of early literature about PCA focused on administration of opioids via an intravenous (IV) route, the principle of patient self-medication on demand has been applied to other classes of medications given by various routes (Tables 1.1 and 1.2).

The concept of self-administered analgesia was introduced in the early 1970s when it became apparent that traditional analgesic therapy involving intramuscular (IM) opioids injected around the clock or as needed resulted in an unacceptable undertreatment of pain in hospitalized patients [1, 2]. Several factors associated with health care providers, analgesics, and patients were identified as responsible for this failure to accomplish adequate pain control with IM opioids (Table 1.3) [3].

In general, a conventional IM analgesic regime is a time-consuming, multi-step process that is controlled and influenced by knowledge and attitudes of health care professionals. It is also characterized by disregard for the patient's judgment about the severity of his or her pain and exclusion of the patient from the decision-making process. Unfortunately, this approach frequently results in repetitive cycles of

Table 1.1   PCA: Classes of Analgesics

Opioids [6, 32]
Local anesthetics [22, 33]
Benzodiazepines [34, 35]
Inhalation agents [36, 37]

Table 1.2   PCA: Routes of Administration

Intravenous [32, 38]
Epidural [22, 39]
Subcutaneous [40, 41]
Oral [42, 43]
Nasal [44, 45]
Inhalational [36, 37]
Sublingual [46, 47]
Intrathecal [48, 49]

Table 1.3   Why As-Needed IM Opioids Are Ineffective Analgesics

Misconceptions about opioids among health care professionals
    Underestimated effective analgesic doses (underprescription)
    Overestimated duration of action (prolonged periods of pain between
        doses)
    Overestimated addictive potential (fear of prescribing and injecting)
    Overestimated risk of respiratory depression (fear of prescribing and
        injecting)
Delay between pain perception and relief (perception → request →
    dispensation → injection → absorption → relief)
Unpredictable opioid blood levels following injection
Interpatient variability of analgesic requirements

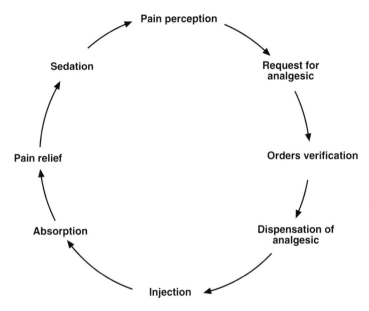

Fig. 1.1   Sequence of events leading to analgesia in traditional IM pain management. Note the delay between pain perception and pain relief.

delayed and incomplete pain relief followed by periods of excessive sedation [4, 5]. On the other hand, PCA places the patient at the center of pain management, thereby allowing him or her to assume a more active role in achieving satisfactory analgesic end points (Figure 1.1).

The technique of IV PCA was described in the late 1960s and early 1970s [6–9]. Prototype models of PCA devices were developed at the same time [6, 8, 9]. Early reports indicated that PCA provided superior analgesia with a lower total opioid dose compared to the traditional IM method. It was also noted that analgesic needs were fairly constant in individual patients but differed significantly among patients [7, 8]. These clinical observations were further corroborated by pharmacologic studies of the dose-concentration–effect curve of opioids. The minimum effective analgesic concentration (MEAC) has been defined as the analgesic blood concentration that is accompanied by total analgesia [10]. The steep slope of the concentration-effect curve has also been demonstrated. A very small decrease in opioid blood level from the MEAC results invariably in severe pain [10]. As predicted by clinical descriptions of PCA, a unique MEAC has been consistently associated with analgesia for each individual, but MEAC varies considerably among patients [10]. Subsequent investigation linked MEAC to individual levels of endorphins and substance P in cerebrospinal fluid, a finding that may account for the substantial interpatient MEAC variability [11].

Clinical and pharmacologic studies suggest that effective opioid analgesia requires dosage individualization to achieve and maintain stable blood opioid levels at or above MEAC [12]. While traditional IM regimens result in prominent peak and trough effects, as evidenced by intermittent periods of pain and sedation, IV PCA tends to minimize wide fluctuations in blood opioid level, thereby decreasing the incidence of side effects and severe pain perception (Figure 1.2).

PCA can be provided using two delivery modes:

1. On demand (fixed or variable dose)
2. On demand + fixed-rate infusion

The simplest system (1), which may be used with any administration route, involves on-demand, fixed dosing. A prescribed constant dose is administered by the patient on demand. Variable-demand–dose IV PCA has been described and compared with fixed-dose PCA [13, 14]. Although variable-demand–dose IV PCA enabled patients to select one of three available doses, the variable-dose IV PCA did not offer any advantage over the conventional fixed-dose PCA [14].

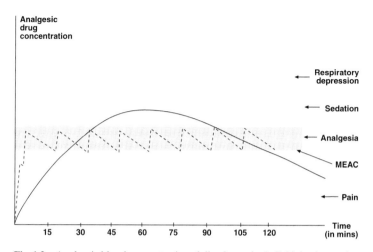

Fig. 1.2 Analgesic blood concentrations following a single IM injection and during PCA. Note the lag period between IM injection (*solid line*) and effective analgesia. PCA (*dotted line*) significantly shortens this delay, provides almost immediate analgesia, and maintains stable analgesic blood level at or above the minimum effective analgesic concentration (MEAC).

The addition of a fixed-rate background infusion to demand dosing creates a separate PCA delivery mode. In general, the use of background infusion results in increased total medication administered without any improvement in pain relief compared to fixed-dose–demand IV or epidural PCA [15–21].

Each PCA prescription should include several essential variables (Table 1.4).

The safety and efficacy of PCA in a variety of acute and chronic pain situations resulted in spread of its use beyond the postanesthe-

Table 1.4   Basic PCA Prescription Variables

Administration route	IV, epidural, subcutaneous, or other
Delivery mode	On-demand dosing with or without background infusion
Drug of choice	Prescribed analgesic, usually opioid or local anesthetic
Loading dose	Initial bolus dose to render patient comfortable
Demand dose	Subsequent bolus doses to maintain patient analgesic
Lockout interval	Minimum time between boluses
Background infusion rate	Rate of continuous infusion, if prescribed
1-hr limit	Total allowable dose of analgesic in 1 hr
4-hr limit	Total allowable dose of analgesic in 4 hrs

sia care unit. PCA has been introduced into labor and delivery suites to provide labor and delivery analgesia as well as post–cesarean section pain relief [22, 23]. Trauma and burn victims have been offered PCA to alleviate their acute pain [24, 25]. Pediatric patients have also benefited from the institution of PCA programs in the postoperative period [26, 27]. The pain of vaso-occlusive crises in sickle-cell disease has been treated using IV PCA [28, 29]. Chronic cancer pain has been safely and effectively managed using IV and subcutaneous PCA [30, 31]. These selected applications of PCA are discussed in the chapters that follow.

REFERENCES

1. Marks RM, Sachar EJ. Undertreatment of medical inpatients with narcotic analgesics. Ann Intern Med 1973;78:173.
2. Donovan M, Dillon P, McGuire L. Incidence and characteristics of pain in a sample of medical-surgical inpatients. Pain 1979;6:249.
3. Smythe M. Patient-controlled analgesia: a review. Pharmacotherapy 1992;12:132.
4. Colier M. Controlling postoperative pain with patient-controlled analgesia. J Prof Nurs 1990;6:121.

5. Paradis A. Patient-controlled analgesia. Can Nurse 1992;88:39.
6. Forrest WH Jr, Smethurst PWR, Kienitz ME. Self-administration of intravenous analgesics. Anesthesiology 1970;33:363.
7. Sechzer PH. Objective measurement of pain. Anesthesiology 1968;29:209.
8. Sechzer PH. Studies in pain with analgesic-demand system. Anesth Analg 1971;50:1.
9. Keeri-Szanto M. Apparatus for demand analgesia. Can Anaesth Soc J 1971;18:581.
10. Austin KL, Stapelton JV, Mather LE. Relationship between blood meperidine concentration and analgesic response: a preliminary report. Anesthesiology 1980;53:460.
11. Tamsen A, Sakaruda T, Wahlstrom A, et al. Postoperative demand for analgesic in relation to individual levels of endorphin and substance P in cerebrospinal fluid. Pain 1982;13:171.
12. Ferrante FM, Covino BG. Patient-Controlled Analgesia: A Historical Perspective. In FM Ferrante, GW Ostheimer, BG Covino (eds), Patient-Controlled Analgesia. Boston: Blackwell, 1990;3.
13. Owen H, Plummer J, Ilsley A, et al. Variable-dose patient-controlled analgesia. A preliminary report. Anaesthesia 1995;50:855.
14. Love DR, Owen H, Ilsley AH, et al. A comparison of variable-dose patient-controlled analgesia with fixed-dose patient-controlled analgesia. Anesth Analg 1996;83:1060.
15. Owen H, Szekely SM, Plummer JL, et al. Variables of patient-controlled analgesia. 2. Concurrent infusion. Anaesthesia 1989;44:11.
16. Russell AW, Owen H, Ilsley AH, et al. Background infusion with patient-controlled analgesia: effect on postoperative oxyhaemoglobin saturation and pain control. Anaesth Intensive Care 1993;21:174.
17. Paech MJ. Patient-controlled epidural analgesia in labour—is a continuous infusion of benefit? Anaesth Intensive Care 1992;20:15.
18. McCoy EP, Furness G, Wright PM. Patient-controlled analgesia with and without background infusion. Analgesia assessed using the demand : delivery ratio. Anaesthesia 1993;48:256.
19. Doyle E, Robinson D, Morton NS. Comparison of patient-controlled analgesia with and without a background infusion after lower abdominal surgery in children. Br J Anaesth 1993;71:670.
20. Ferrante FM, Rosinia FA, Gordon C, Datta S. The role of continuous background infusions in patient-controlled epidural analgesia for labor and delivery. Anesth Analg 1994;79:80.

21. Vercauteren MP, Coppejans HC, ten Broecke PW, et al. Epidural sufentanil for postoperative patient-controlled analgesia (PCA) with or without background infusion: a double-blind comparison. Anesth Analg 1995;80:76.

22. Gambling DR, Yu P, Cole C, et al. A comparative study of patient controlled epidural analgesia (PCEA) and continuous infusion epidural analgesia (CIEA) during labour. Can J Anaesth 1988;35:249.

23. Parker RK, White PF. Epidural patient-controlled analgesia: an alternative to IV patient-controlled analgesia for pain relief after cesarean delivery. Anesth Analg 1992;75:245.

24. Hauer M, Cram E, Titler M, et al. Intravenous patient-controlled analgesia in critically ill postoperative/trauma patients: research-based practice recommendations. Dimens Crit Care Nurs 1995;14:144.

25. Kinsella J, Glavin R, Reid WH. Patient-controlled analgesia for burn patients: a preliminary report. Burns 1988;14:500.

26. Doyle E, Harper I, Morton NS. Patient-controlled analgesia with low dose background infusions after lower abdominal surgery in children. Br J Anaesth 1993;71:818.

27. Berde CB, Lehn BM, Yee JD, et al. Patient-controlled analgesia in children and adolescents: a randomized, prospective comparison with IM administration of morphine for postoperative analgesia. J Pediatr 1991;118:460.

28. McPherson E, Perlin E, Finke H, et al. Patient-controlled analgesia in patients with sickle cell vaso-occlusive crisis. Am J Med Sci 1990;299:10.

29. Shapiro BS, Cohen DE, Howe CJ. Patient-controlled analgesia for sickle-cell–related pain. J Pain Symptom Manage 1993;8(1):22.

30. Citron ML, Kalra JM, Seltzer VL, et al. Patient-controlled analgesia for cancer pain: a long-term study of inpatient and outpatient use. Cancer Invest 1992;10:335.

31. Swanson G, Smith J, Bulich R, et al. Patient-controlled analgesia for chronic cancer pain in the ambulatory setting: a report of 117 patients. J Clin Oncol 1989;7:1903.

32. Bahar M, Rosen M, Vickers MD. Self-administered nalbuphine, morphine and pethidine. Comparison, by intravenous route, following cholecystectomy. Anaesthesia 1985;40:529.

33. Gambling DR, McMorland GH, Yu P, Laszlo C. Comparison of patient-controlled epidural analgesia and conventional intermittent "top-up" injections during labor. Anesth Analg 1990;70:256.

34. Zacharias M, Hunter KM, Luyk NH. Patient-controlled sedation using midazolam. Br J Oral Maxillofac Surg 1994;32:168.

35. Bernard JM, Faintreny A, Lienhart A, Souron-R. Patient-controlled pre-medication by i.v. midazolam for ambulatory surgery. Acta Anaesthesiol Scand 1996;40:331.

36. Stewart RD, Paris PM, Stoy WA, Cannon G. Patient-controlled inhalational analgesia in prehospital care: a study of side-effects and feasibility. Crit Care Med 1983;11:851.

37. Wee MY, Hasan MA, Thomas TA. Isoflurane in labour. Anaesthesia 1993;48:369.

38. Bollish SJ, Collins CL, Kirking DM, Bartlett RH. Efficacy of patient-controlled versus conventional analgesia for postoperative pain. Clin Pharm 1985;4:48.

39. Sjöstrom S, Hartvig D, Tamsen A. Patient-controlled analgesia with extradural morphine or pethidine. Br J Anaesth 1988;60:358.

40. Urquhart ML, Klapp K, White PF. Patient-controlled analgesia: a comparison of IV versus subcutaneous hydromorphone. Anesthesiology 1988;69:428.

41. White PF. Subcutaneous-PCA: an alternative to IV-PCA for postoperative pain management. Clin J Pain 1990;6:297.

42. Karpman RR, Bontrager J, Quinn P. Pain clinic #12. The use of a self-administration system for oral analgesics on an orthopaedic service. Orthop Rev 1989;18:120.

43. Litman RS, Shapiro BS. Oral patient-controlled analgesia in adolescents. J Pain Symptom Manage 1992;7(2):78.

44. Striebel HW, Bonillo B, Schwagmeier R, et al. Self-administered intranasal meperidine for postoperative pain management. Can J Anaesth 1995;42:287.

45. Striebel HW, Oelmann T, Spies C, et al. Patient-controlled intranasal analgesia: a method for noninvasive postoperative pain management. Anesth Analg 1996;83:548.

46. Shah MV, Jones DI, Rosen M. "Patient demand" postoperative analgesia with buprenorphine. Comparison between sublingual and i.m. administration. Br J Anaesth 1986;58:508.

47. Witjes WP, Crul BJ, Vollaard EJ, et al. Application of sublingual buprenorphine in combination with naproxen or paracetamol for postoperative pain relief in cholecystectomy patients in a double-blind study. Acta Anaesthesiol Scand 1992;36:323.

48. Hardy PA, Wells JC. Patient-controlled intrathecal morphine for cancer pain. A method used to assess morphine requirements and bolus doses. Clin J Pain 1990;6:57.

49. Devulder J. PCA and cancer pain. Acta Anaesthesiol Belg 1992;43:53.

2

Pharmacology and Pharmacokinetics of Opioids for Patient-Controlled Analgesia

Despite recent advances in anesthesia, many patients are treated suboptimally for postoperative pain [1]. Patients often receive less than one-half of what is actually needed to relieve their pain. The primary reasons may relate to lack of information about analgesic drugs and misconceptions about their potency, duration of action, side effects, and addictive potential. Additionally, pharmacokinetic and pharmacodynamic variability contributes to the difficulty in predicting the analgesic requirement for any given patient. PCA systems are designed to accommodate the wide range of analgesia requirements that can be anticipated when managing acute pain.

OPIOIDS FOR PCA

There are a large number of analgesic drugs that can be used with PCA therapy (Table 2.1). The ideal characteristics of opioids for PCA therapy are listed in Table 2.2. Morphine and meperidine have been the most widely used; hydromorphone and oxymorphone are excellent alternatives. The physicochemical properties of morphine, meperidine, and fentanyl are listed in Table 2.3.

Morphine

Morphine is a naturally existing alkaloid derived from the opium poppy plant and is a prototypic μ-agonist available in oral, paren-

**Table 2.1   Opioid Preparations Currently Available
for Postoperative Analgesia**

Agonists	Morphine
	Hydromorphone
	Oxymorphone
	Meperidine
	Methadone
	Fentanyl
	Sufentanil
	Alfentanil
Partial agonists	Codeine
	Propoxyphene
	Buprenorphine
Agonist-antagonists	Pentazocine
	Nalbuphine
	Butorphanol
	Dezocine
	Bremazocine

Table 2.2   Ideal Characteristics of Opioids for PCA Systems

Rapid onset of analgesic action
Highly efficient in relieving pain
Intermediate duration of action (i.e., ability to control titration)
Do not lead to tolerance or dependence
Minimal side effects and adverse drug reactions
Noncumulative

teral, and rectal forms. It is the least lipid soluble of all opioids and is
metabolized principally in the liver. The main metabolites are
morphine-3-glucuronide, which has no analgesic action, and
morphine-6-glucuronide (M6G), which is an analgesic twice as
potent as morphine. The glucuronides are primarily excreted via the
kidneys. Renal impairment leads to accumulation of these metabolites. Less than 10% of morphine is excreted unchanged by the kid-

Table 2.3   Physicochemical and Pharmacokinetic Properties of Opioids for PCA

Opioids	Partition Coefficient at pH = 7.4*	pKa	Percent Unionized at pH = 7.4	Percent Unbound at pH = 7.4	Vd (liters/kg)	TBCL (liters/min)	Binding Affinity
Morphine	1	7.9	5	80	3.2	0.8–1.2	5.7
Meperidine	21	8.7	24	60	3.8	0.4–0.8	193
Fentanyl	950	8.4	9	20	4.1	0.8–1.5	1.6

V_d = volume of distribution; TBCL = total body clearance; pK_a = dissociation constant.
*n-octanol; pH 7.4 buffer.

neys. The half-life of morphine is not increased in patients with reduced renal function, although there may be an apparent prolonged morphine effect due to accumulation of M6G.

Morphine may be given by IM, IV, subcutaneous, oral, rectal, epidural, and intrathecal routes. Dose ranges and intervals vary according to the route of administration. Slow- or sustained-release preparations of oral morphine are available for the treatment of chronic and cancer pain and need only be given two or three times daily. The slower onset and longer duration of action of the sustained-release formulations make fast titration of the drug impossible, and it is therefore unsuitable for treatment of acute pain.

After IV administration, morphine is rapidly distributed to tissues and organs. Ninety-six percent to 98% of the drug is cleared from the plasma within 10 minutes of administration [2]. Therefore, plasma concentrations do not correlate with the pharmacologic activity of the opioid [3]. In fact, the analgesic effects of morphine may not be apparent during the time of peak plasma concentrations after IV injection.

Meperidine

Meperidine is a member of the phenylpiperidine series of opioid μ-agonists. After IV injection, meperidine is rapidly and extensively distributed to extravascular tissues. Distribution is complete in 30–45 minutes (morphine requires 10 minutes). The elimination half-life is 3.5–4.0 hours [4]. Approximately 60% of the drug is bound to plasma protein. It is extensively metabolized in the liver to normeperidine and hydrolyzed to meperidinic acid. Less than 5% is excreted unchanged in the urine. Urinary acidification can speed elimination [5]. Meperidine is seven to 10 times less potent than morphine when given parenterally. In analgesic doses, it has no cardiovascular effects. In large doses (e.g., 2.5 mg/kg), however, myocardial contractility and stroke volume are reduced and filling pressures are elevated [6]. As opposed to other opioids, meperidine causes mydriasis, tachycardia, and less smooth muscle spasm

Table 2.4   Guidelines for Bolus Doses and Lockout Intervals for Opioids via a PCA System[*]

Drug (drug concentration as available for PCA use)	Bolus Dose (mg)	Lockout Interval (min)
Morphine (1 mg/ml)	0.5–3.0	5–20
Meperidine (10 mg/ml)	5–30	5–15
Hydromorphone (0.2 mg/ml)	0.1–0.6	5–15
Oxymorphone (0.25 mg/ml)	0.1–0.6	5–15
Fentanyl (10 mg/ml)	0.02–0.10	3–10
Nalbuphine (1 mg/ml)	1–5	5–15

[*]Assuming an adult of average body weight.

because of its moderate atropine-like qualities. Additionally, meperidine has modest local anesthetic properties. A syndrome of hyperpyrexia, convulsions, coma, and hypertension or hypotension has been reported in patients maintained on monoamine oxidase inhibitors and subsequently given meperidine [7–9].

Meperidine can be administered via oral, parenteral, and intrathecal routes. The intramuscular dose is 75–100 mg every 2–4 hours. Meperidine infusions of 0.5–1.5 mg/kg administered as a loading dose over 30–60 minutes followed by infusion of 0.25–0.75 mg per minute may be used [10]. PCA doses are given in Table 2.4.

Normeperidine Toxicity

Normeperidine toxicity (Table 2.5) may develop in patients receiving large doses or continuous infusions or in those with renal impairment. It is suggested that young adult, healthy patients with normal renal function not receive more than 1,000 mg of meperidine in the first 24 hours [11]. These limits should be reduced by one-half in the elderly and in patients with renal impairment.

In patients with cirrhosis and impaired liver function, normeperidine is produced more slowly but accumulates for a longer period, placing the patient at risk for systemic toxicity.

Table 2.5   Normeperidine Toxicity

Effects of normeperidine	Analgesia (μ-receptor–mediated)
	Central nervous system excitation
	Elimination half-life of 15–20 hours
Signs and symptoms	Anxiety, agitation, mood changes, tremors, twitching, myoclonic jerks, convulsions
Treatment	No specific treatment
	Discontinue meperidine
	Substitute an alternative opioid
	Symptomatic treatment of effects
	Wait
Caution	Do not administer naloxone

Hydromorphone

Hydromorphone is derived by replacing the hydroxyl group with an oxygen atom at the C6 position of the phenanthrene nucleus. Hydromorphone is six times more potent than morphine (Table 2.6). Its lipid solubility is 10 times greater than that of morphine. When administered using IV injection, hydromorphone has a rapid distribution phase similar to that of morphine. Approximately 90% is lost from the plasma in 10 minutes. Also, as with morphine, hydromorphone elimination depends on tissue uptake with subsequent slow release from tissue to plasma [12]. Unlike morphine, hydromorphone has no active metabolites and is thus the opioid of choice in patients with renal failure. The oral analgesic is one-fifth as potent as the parenteral form. As expected from its close structural relationship to morphine, hydromorphone has a similar pharmacodynamic profile and similar clinical effects and complications. Although unproved, anecdotal reports claim a reduced incidence of nausea, vomiting, respiratory depression, urinary retention, and constipation when hydromorphone is used for pain. Recommended bolus doses of hydromorphone for PCA systems are given in Table 2.4.

Table 2.6   Analgesic Equivalents, Half-Lives, and Durations of Action of Opioids Compared to Morphine

Opioid	Intramuscular Analgesic (mg)	Oral Equivalents (mg)	Plasma Half-Life (hrs)	Duration of Action (hrs)
Morphine	10	30–60	2.0–3.5	2–3
Meperidine	75	300	3–4	3–5
Hydromorphone	1.5	6–8	2–3	2–3
Oxymorphone	1.0	—	2–3	2–3
Fentanyl	0.1	—	3–4	2–3
Nalbuphine	10	—	3–6	4–5

Fentanyl

Fentanyl is a synthetic congener of meperidine and belongs to the phenylpiperidine series. It is 80–100 times more potent than morphine. Fentanyl is a highly lipid-soluble opioid that does not release histamine even at high doses. It has a more rapid onset of action than morphine, and single doses have a short duration of action because of rapid tissue uptake. Fentanyl is more suited for intraoperative analgesia than for postoperative analgesia. The metabolites are inactive.

Nalbuphine

Nalbuphine is a semisynthetic mixed agonist-antagonist that is chemically related to oxymorphone and naloxone. It is metabolized in the liver. The major metabolite is an inactive glucuronide conjugate. Fecal excretion is the primary source of elimination of nalbuphine and its metabolites. Only 7% of a single dose of nalbuphine is excreted in the urine. The elimination half-life ($t_{1/2\beta}$) is 3–6 hours (see Table 2.6).

Nalbuphine is a partial κ-receptor agonist and μ-antagonist. It has a ceiling effect on analgesia: At doses greater than 0.45 mg/kg, no further analgesia or respiratory depression is noted. Sedation and diaphoresis are the most common side effects (33%) [13]. In contrast to other drugs in its class, nalbuphine produces less dysphoria and fewer cardiovascular effects (i.e., no increase in systemic blood pressure, pulmonary artery pressure, or heart rate). Nalbuphine crosses the placenta to cause a newborn concentration of 0.33–6.00 times the maternal concentration. There are no known adverse effects on the neonate. However, experience with nalbuphine for IV PCA and epidural analgesia during labor and delivery is limited [14, 15]. The usual adult dose is 10 mg every 3–6 hours. No more than 160 mg should be administered in 24 hours.

For labor analgesia, nalbuphine can be administered via PCA as follows:

- Loading dose 2–4 mg
- Demand dose 1 mg
- Lockout interval 6–10 minutes

In other surgical categories associated with more severe pain, nalbuphine PCA may not be adequate and should be replaced by a μ-agonist drug.

Oxymorphone

Oxymorphone is synthesized by adding a hydroxyl group to the C14 position of hydromorphone. When administered parenterally, it is 10 times as potent as morphine (see Table 2.6). The oral to parenteral potency ratio for oxymorphone itself is 1 to 6. The clinical pharmacologic profile is similar to morphine except that there is an enhanced addiction potential and no histamine release. The pharmacokinetics of oxymorphone are not fully understood. Because of its potency, short duration of action, and lack of histamine release, oxymorphone has been used for IV PCA [16] and subcutaneous PCA (SC-PCA) (Table 2.7) [17].

Table 2.7 Guidelines for Opioid Administration via Subcutaneous PCA

Drug (concentration)	Demand Dose	Lockout Interval (min)
Morphine (50 mg/ml)	0.2 ml = 1 mg	10
Hydromorphone (1.0 mg/ml)	0.2 ml = 0.2 mg	15
Oxymorphone (1.5 mg/ml)	0.2 ml = 0.3 mg	10

Note: Compared with IV PCA, more concentrated solutions and smaller dose volumes are used in subcutaneous PCA to minimize the fluid volume administered.

PHARMACOKINETICS OF PATIENT-CONTROLLED OPIOID ANALGESICS

For an opioid to be effective it must reach a certain concentration in the blood (enteral and parenteral routes only). The effective range of blood concentration varies four- to fivefold between patients, and the amount of opioid that each patient requires also varies according to the severity of the pain stimulus. Thus, titration of opioids is needed to individualize treatment. Enter the PCA concept, which allows for and accommodates interpatient painful stimuli variability. Although the pharmacokinetic principles are important and may explain some of the drug actions, the PCA concept also encompasses the kinetics of pharmacodynamics.

Minimum Effective Analgesic Concentration

Minimum effective analgesic concentration (Table 2.8) is the lowest blood concentration of opioid that will produce analgesia. Below this level a patient will experience no pain relief, and above it there will be increasing analgesia (*analgesic corridor*) and an increasing possibility of side effects. In reality, the boundaries are not clear cut and side effects may occur before effective analgesia is achieved. For each patient, the key is to find and maintain the effective blood level within this corridor (Figure 2.1). A change in pain intensity may shift the corridor and require modification of opioid dose.

Table 2.8   Median Minimum Effective Analgesic Concentrations

Morphine	16 ng/ml
Meperidine	455 ng/ml
Fentanyl	1 ng/ml
Alfentanil	10 ng/ml

Note: These opioids are similar in that these data cannot be applied to any individual patient. That is a drawback of the pharmacokinetically planned pain treatment but not of PCA, which takes into account interpatient variability and varying pain intensity.

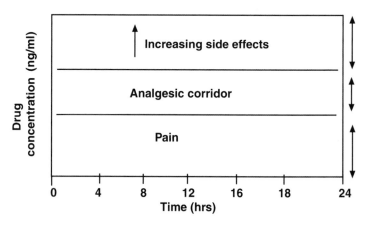

Fig. 2.1   Analgesic corridor.

To titrate opioid analgesia to suit each patient, appropriate doses and dose intervals must be ordered. In addition, end points that indicate adequate or excessive doses must be monitored.

Dose Range and Interval

Dose range should be the average for the age of the patient and varies according to the route of administration. The goal of the dose interval is to allow the previous dose to have an effect before another dose is given and to indicate how long a single dose can be expected to have an effect. Thus, the time taken for the drug to reach its peak effect as well as the duration of action of the drug must be taken into account.

Onset of Action and Maximum Effect

The time necessary for an opioid to reach maximum blood concentration depends primarily on the route of administration. The time necessary to achieve maximum effect, however, depends on the time it takes the drug to cross the blood-brain barrier and bind to the opioid receptors (Figures 2.2 and 2.3) in the central nervous system. Morphine, which is the least lipid-soluble opioid, may have a latency of up to 15 minutes for maximum effect (Table 2.9). Similarly, alfentanil (not shown in the table) may have a rapid onset and short duration of action.

Duration of Action

The duration of action of an opioid depends on a number of factors, including the amount given; the route of administration; the pharmacokinetic characteristics of the drug, such as absorption, rate of distribution to different tissues (including receptors), and rate of dissociation from receptors; and the $t_{1/2\beta}$. The $t_{1/2\beta}$ indicates the time needed for the body to metabolize and excrete the drug. It alone does not determine duration of action; it is only the time taken for the blood concentration of the drug to change by 50%.

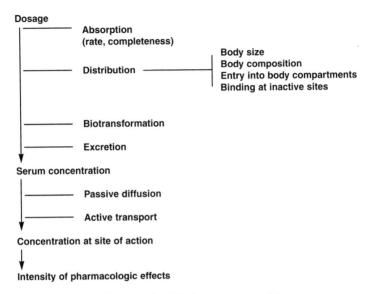

Fig. 2.2   Factors influencing the clinical dose response of drugs.

The drugs are metabolized to a form that is more easily excreted. In the case of opioids, the liver is the primary site of metabolism and the kidneys the primary route of excretion of metabolites. It is possible to make some general predictions regarding how an opioid is likely to behave in the PCA environment by considering pharmacokinetic characteristics.

OBJECTIVES OF PCA

The objectives of PCA are as follows:

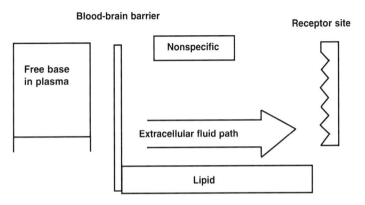

Fig. 2.3   Factors influencing the diffusion of an opioid from the plasma to receptor sites in the brain.

Table 2.9   Pharmacokinetic Characteristics Influencing Clearance for Selected Opioids

	Morphine	Meperidine	Fentanyl
Octanol/water for free base	6	525	11,220
Unbound percentage	70	30	16
Free base percentage	23	7	9
Diffusible base percentage	16.1	2.5	1.4
Lipid diffusing index	1	13.6	162
Initial V_d (liters)	23	88	60
Total V_d (liters)	224	305	335
Initial half-life (min)	1.7	7.1	4.1
Terminal half-life (min)	177	222	185
Clearance (ml/min)	1,050	1,020	1,530

V_d = volume of distribution.

1. To achieve effective analgesia as rapidly as possible with the minimum dose of drug so that only the desired effect (analgesia without unacceptable respiratory depression) results.
2. To maintain continuously effective analgesia for extended periods, during which the patient should be able to maintain a normal sleep pattern.

Based on these premises and the application of pharmacokinetic data, morphine and meperidine are the opioids of choice for use in the PCA model. During the initial "achieve-analgesia" phase, when the patient's blood is drug free, each demand dose will behave like a small bolus, with a rapid rise followed by a rapid decline, due mainly to distribution (Figure 2.4). Eventually, a steady state will develop, with input balancing elimination and the plasma concentration oscillating within a steady-state level. In the case of morphine, there will be little immediate effect due to onset latency, but analgesia develops progressively.

When using fentanyl or alfentanil, each peak will result in the rapid onset of a brief period of analgesia, with redistribution from the brain to other tissues. To maintain a steady state, the initial dose frequency must be staggered. Contrast this with morphine, where, after analgesia is initially achieved, the dose frequency may have to be spread out to prevent an "overshoot" of both concentration and effect.

If the patient falls asleep and stops demanding the drug (Figure 2.5), the plasma concentration will fall below the analgesic corridor and, depending on the choice of agent, result in severe discomfort on arousal. Hence, some physicians prefer simultaneous infusions that can sustain the plasma concentrations during such periods.

Opioid pharmacokinetics must be considered when selecting a drug for PCA. At the same time, it must be understood that the differences between patients who are suffering from pain may be explicable in physical or psychological terms, but these explanations do not permit the application of gross blood kinetics to any

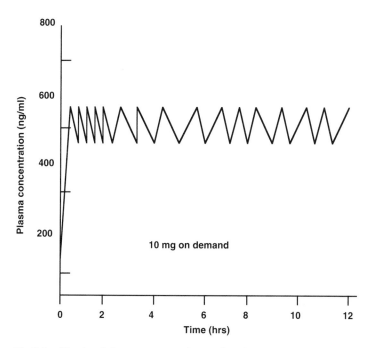

Fig. 2.4 Simulated plasma concentration predicted by a pharmacokinetic model for meperidine (10 mg is administered by IV whenever the plasma concentration falls to 450 ng/ml).

individual patient. Bearing these points in mind, PCA can be regarded as a promising concept to overcome the problems of individual variability and unforeseeable drug interactions with respect to pain sensation.

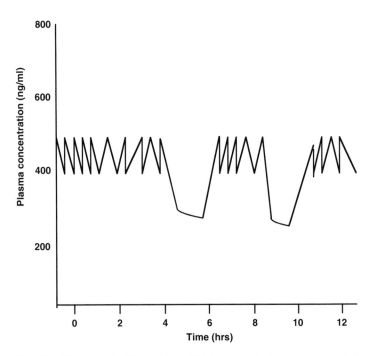

Fig. 2.5   The model for Figure 2.4 in which two periods of sleep are simulated.

REFERENCES

1. Carr DB, Jacox AK, Chapman RC, et al. Acute Pain Management.
   Operative or Medical Procedures and Trauma, Clinical Practice Guide-
   lines #92-0032. Rockville, MD: Agency for Health Care Policy and
   Research. Public Health Service, U.S. Department of Health and
   Human Services, 1992.
2. Murphy MR, Hug CC Jr. Pharmacokinetics of intravenous morphine in

patients anesthetized with enflurane-nitrous oxide. Anesthesiology 1981;54:187.

3. Hug CC, Murphy MR, Rigel EP, Olson WA. Pharmacokinetics of morphine injected intravenously into the anesthetized dog. Anesthesiology 1981;54:38.

4. Koska AJ, Kramer WC, Romagnoli A, et al. Pharmacokinetics of high dose meperidine in surgical patients. Anesth Analg 1981;60:8.

5. Veerback RK, Branch RA, Wilkinson GR. Meperidine disposition in main influence of urinary pH and route of administration. Clin Pharm Ther 1981;30:619.

6. Strauer BE. Contractile responses to morphine, piritramide, meperidine and fentanyl: a comparative study of effects on the isolated ventricular myocardium. Anesthesiology 1972;37:304.

7. Brown TCK. Cass NM. Beware—the use of MAO inhibitors is increasing again. Anaesth Intensive Care 1979;7:65.

8. Lewis E. Hyperpyrexia with antidepressant drugs. Br Med J 1965;2:1671.

9. Rogers KJ. Role of brain monoamines on the interaction between pethidine and tranylcypromine. Eur J Pharmacol 1971;14:86.

10. Stapleton JV, Austin KL, Mather LE. A pharmacokinetic approach to post-operative pain: continuous infusion of pethidine. Anesth Intensive Care 1979;7:25.

11. Stone PA, Macintyre PE, Jarvis DA. Norpethidine toxicity and patient controlled analgesia. Br J Anaesth 1993;71:738.

12. Hill HF, Coda BA, Aleira TA, Scaffer R. Multiple dose evaluations of intravenous hydromorphone pharmacokinetics in normal human subjects. Anesth Analg 1991;72:330.

13. Errick JK, Heel RC. Nalbuphine: a preliminary review of its pharmacological properties and therapeutic efficacy. Drugs 1983;26:191.

14. Lehman KA, Tenbulis B. Patient controlled analgesia with nalbuphine, a new narcotic agonist antagonist for the treatment of postoperative pain. Eur J Clin Pharmacol 1986;31:261.

15. Sprigg E, Otton PE. Nalbuphine vs meperidine for post-operative analgesia: a double-blind comparison with patient controlled analgesic technique. Can Anesth Soc J 1983;303:517.

16. Sinatra RS, Lodge K, Sibert K, et al. A comparison of morphine, meperidine and oxymorphone as utilized in patient controlled analgesia following cesarean delivery. Anesthesiology 1989;70:585.

17. Sinatra RS, Hamsor DN. Oxymorphone in patient controlled analgesia. Clin Pharm 1989;8:541.

3

Equipment and Record Keeping

PCA apparatus was first constructed by the Newcastle group in 1976 [1]. Voice-prompted PCA equipment using tape synchronization was first used successfully by Hull in 1979 [2]. It used a continuous infusion with demand dosing and was very popular with nurses and patients. A microprocessor-operated, on-demand analgesia computer, which used an automatic syringe and higher level of dose control, was developed by Janssen Scientific Instruments in Belgium [1]. The progressive improvements in PCA drug-delivery systems have led to the development of the present product, which is very safe, reliable, and easy to use. The conventional pain-control feedback loop (Figure 3.1) was modified to develop a PCA feedback loop (Figure 3.2) by eliminating the intervention of nursing staff and thus giving the control of pain medication back to the patient.

The first commercially available PCA device was developed by Evans et al. in 1976 and called the Cardiff Palliator [3]. Tables 3.1 through 3.3 discuss important features of PCA equipment. Based on these features, various commercially available PCA devices have been developed (Table 3.4). The following section lists some of the important features of these devices.

FEATURES OF SPECIFIC PCA DEVICES

Cardiff Palliator

The advantages of the Cardiff Palliator are as follows:

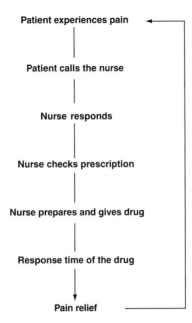

Fig 3.1   The conventional pain-control feedback loop.

- Line-powered syringe pump
- Infusion rate, desired dose, and lockout interval are programmable
- Requires the button to be pressed twice in rapid succession for dose delivery
- Uses a 30-ml syringe
- Lockout period is identified by a constant yellow indicator light
- Infusion of the dose is indicated by an audible tone
- Alarm sounds when syringe is empty

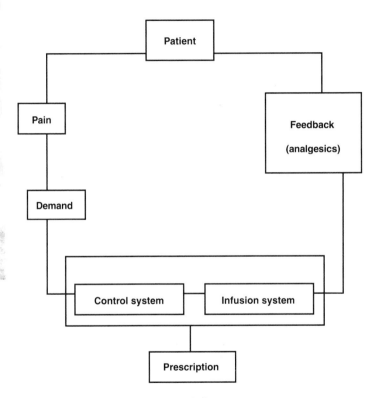

Fig. 3.2   Feedback loop used for PCA devices.

Table 3.1   Basic Requirements of PCA Devices

Deliver an accurate present bolus with or without continuous infusion
Deliver a bolus over a short period of time
Provide an accurate lockout interval
Prolonged operational ability
Patient-friendly activation system

Table 3.2   Safety Requirements of PCA Devices

Explicit, easy, logical, and sequential program designed to minimize
    errors in prescription
Protection from overinfusion
Time-period drug limit to allow a shorter lockout interval while prevent-
    ing drug overdose
User-friendly
Password mechanism program access to prevent unauthorized changes
    in prescription
Locking device to secure the drug reservoir
Frequent supervision
Frequent documentation of the drug use
Tamper-resistant delivery system with minimal amount of drug tubing

**Table 3.3   PCA Device Features That Promote
Flexibility and Effectiveness**

Occlusion alarm
Refill alert alarm
Continuous infusion
Delivery of variable bolus volume
Ability to retrieve data
Audible signals for patient reassurance
Option to disable alarms
Ability to retain a hard copy permanently
Lightweight
Disposable reservoirs and delivery system
Antireflux delivery system using one-way valve mechanism

Table 3.4   Commercially Manufactured PCA Devices

Cardiff Palliator (Graseby Dynamics, England)
Graseby PCAs (Graseby Dynamics, England)
Prominject (Pharmacia AB, Sweden)
Abbott PCA device (Abbott Laboratories, North Chicago, IL)
Bard Harvard/Baxter PCA device (C.R. Bard, Inc., Murray Hill, NJ)
Becton-Dickinson IVAC PCA device (B-D Infusion Systems, Lincoln
   Park, NJ)
Pharmacia Deltac CADD PCA (Pharmacia Deltac, St. Paul, MN)

CADD = continuous and drug on-demand; IVAC = intravenous accurate control.

The disadvantages of the Cardiff Palliator are as follows:

- Thumb wheel switches are not tamper proof
- Interruption of the main power supply wipes out the lockout
  interval
- Machine does not lock and is not protected from theft of the drug
  syringe

Graseby PCA

The advantages of the Graseby PCA are as follows:

- Uses standard 60-ml Becton-Dickinson (BD) syringe
- Uses rechargeable batteries
- Requires a key for programming
- Requires confirmation of drug concentration
- Requires confirmation of prescription

The disadvantages of the Graseby PCA are as follows:

- Each use, successful or not, is accompanied by an audible sound
  based on the lockout interval

Prominject

The advantages of the Prominject are as follows:

- Delivers analgesics as well as other critical care drugs
- Microprocessor-controlled, programmable infusion pump with three separate modules for patient control, consecutive infusion, and constant infusion
- Uses 20-ml BD Luer-Lok syringe
- Syringe placed in a strong plastic cover
- Acoustic and diagnostic line occlusion and empty syringe and low battery alarm
- Alarm conditions interrupt drug delivery
- Lightweight
- Can use direct power supply or rechargeable battery supply
- Can deliver split incremental doses (bolus dose and tail dose)
- Can administer bolus doses over a specific period of time
- Cover is locked by a key that also electronically locks keyboard
- Has a memory and printer for data retrieval
- Can be mounted on a tabletop or an infusion stand

Abbott PCA Device

The advantages of the Abbott PCA device are as follows:

- Uses combined microprocessor and stepping motor technology
- Can deliver intermittent demand and/or continuous infusions
- Uses a 30-ml BD Luer-Lok syringe
- Lightweight and portable
- Computerized volumetric pump
- Lockable security device to prevent unauthorized access
- Mandatory lockout of 5 minutes after every use
- Four-hour dose limit ranging from 5 to 30 ml
- Thirty-six–hour memory

The disadvantages of the Abbott PCA device are as follows:

- Features a purge facility, which is a source of danger to the patient if instructions to disconnect are ignored
- Patient switch resembles a nurse call button

Bard Harvard Devices

There are three main Bard Harvard devices: (1) Bard Harvard PCA device, (2) Bard PCA I device, and (3) Bard Ambulatory PCA device.

Bard Harvard PCA Device

The advantages of the Bard Harvard PCA device are as follows:

- Portable syringe infusion device
- Can give both continuous and intermittent drug infusions
- Uses microprocessor-controlled stepping motor
- Alarms for low battery, excessive pressure, empty syringe, and control circuit failure
- Uses a 60-ml BD Plastipak or Monoject syringe
- Uses an alphanumeric crystal display panel
- Stores data hour by hour for up to 48 hours
- Can use a printer
- Requires three-digit security access code to change the prescription or retrieve the data
- Pole mounted
- Uses Y-type Harvard dispensing tubing with antireflux valve
- Records the total number of attempts made during lockout period to adjust the dose

Bard PCA I Device

The advantages of the Bard PCA I device are as follows:

- Simplified version of Bard Harvard PCA device
- Lightweight

- Limited in flexibility of dosage and delay compared to Bard Harvard PCA device
- Uses D-size alkaline batteries
- Automatically calculates hourly maximum limit based on the prescription

Bard Ambulatory PCA Device

The advantages of the Bard Ambulatory PCA device are as follows:

- Very lightweight
- Worn by the patient or attached to a pole
- Uses a 9-V battery
- All the features of the original Bard Harvard PCA device
- Large drug volume capacity
- Uses special microbore tubing

Baxter PCA Infusor

The advantages of the Baxter PCA Infusor are as follows:

- Nonelectronic and fully disposable
- Consists of a 30- to 60-ml plastic balloon reservoir that fills the injection reservoir slowly
- Programmed to give a fixed volume of the drug from the wrist band reservoir
- Requires change in the drug concentration to change the dose
- Can be programmed for a 6-minute or longer delay to refill the injection reservoir
- Very inexpensive and extremely light

The disadvantages of the Baxter PCA Infusor are as follows:

- Less flexibility
- No fail-safe mechanism
- No memory or retrievable data

Becton-Dickinson IVAC PCA Device

The advantages of the Becton-Dickinson IVAC PCA device are as follows:

- Lightweight and portable
- Uses four D batteries
- Computerized syringe-based pump
- Simplified liquid crystal displays alphanumeric user-friendly panel
- Uses standard 20- to 60-ml disposable BD syringes
- Has a clear tamper-proof plastic cover
- Uses standard antireflux microbore tubing
- Has up to 99 hours of operational memory

Pharmacia Deltac CADD PCA Device

The advantages of the Pharmacia Deltac CADD PCA device are as follows:

- Small and portable
- Can be used outside the hospital
- Uses prefilled sterilized disposable cassettes
- Low volume, low battery, and mechanical failure alarms
- Can deliver analgesics continuously and on demand

SUMMARY

The rational and intelligent use of PCA devices allows the safe and effective delivery of opioids to the patient on demand. PCA devices can be used to control acute and chronic pain depending on the physician's and patient's choice.

RECORD KEEPING

Because the implementation of a PCA program starts with the purchase of equipment, the record keeping starts in the biomedical or engineering department. The equipment should be delivered to the appropriate department to be inspected, marked, and tested before being delivered to the user department. The equipment should be added to the hospital equipment inventory. Once the equipment is delivered to the user department, a formal record of the equipment must be maintained. The units should be numbered in a convenient manner so that they can be traced easily. It is recommended that a logbook be maintained in the user department so that a record of the equipment number can be maintained.

The nursing staff plays an important role in maintaining these records. If the postanesthesia care unit (PACU) is the point of origin for the PCA device, the logbook should be maintained by PACU staff. The logbook should contain equipment and patient information. A record of the patient's name, hospital number, and destination in the hospital should be maintained so that the equipment can be easily traced. Before putting the equipment to use, hospital staff directly involved in PCA should be trained. It is important for the staff to understand the principle of PCA. A hospital-wide policy should be issued that contains information about the equipment and instructions on how to use it. It should also include the various drugs to be used in the PCA device. The policy should be easily obtainable in all areas of use. A frequent staff education session should be conducted for troubleshooting purposes. The education should be a two-way process: staff and patients learning from instructors and instructors learning from staff experiences and patient feedback.

Because opioids are used for pain management in PCA devices and they have an abuse potential, it is important to maintain a record of the opioids dispensed. Cooperation with the pharmacy staff is convenient for the anesthesiologist for keeping records of dispensed and used drugs [4]. Various pilot programs have shown that pharmacists can fill a number of key roles in the implementation of PCA programs [5, 6].

Table 3.5   Guidelines for a Prescription Form for PCA

Patient information
Date and time of initiation of therapy
Any drug allergies
Particular opioid and concentration to be used
Loading dose
PCA dose
Lockout interval
Basal rate (if being used)
1- or 4-hr dose limit
Serious side effects and their treatment
Person to notify in case of emergency

A PCA order prescription form has proven beneficial for physicians, nurses, and pharmacists [4]. Table 3.5 lists some important information to be included in a prescription form. Figure 3.3 provides a possible prototype developed at Lincoln Medical and Mental Health Center, Bronx, New York.

Drug compatibility forms are important and should be provided by the pharmacy department at the user site. Information can also be distributed to all patients receiving PCA. The important drugs and their compatibility with commonly used medications for PCA are listed in Table 3.6.

Because the implementation and success of a PCA program depend on the combined efforts of various health care professionals, it is important to have input from all health care professionals involved in pain management. Proper record maintenance can avoid problems such as lost equipment, unaccounted drugs, and nonfunctioning equipment.

PCA Orders

Date: _____

Time: _____

Drug: (Check one box)   Mode:

[ ] Morphine 1 mg/ml   [ ] PCA only

[ ] Meperidine 10 mg/ml   [ ] BASAL/PCA

[ ] Other (specify) _____ Concentration _____   [ ] Continuous only

Bolus dose (optional): _____ mg   Time: _____

PCA dose: _____ mg   i.e., _____ ml

Lockout interval (delay): _____ minutes

Basal rate: _____ mg/hr, i.e., _____ _____ ml/hr

Continuous infusion (optional): _____ mg/hr, i.e., _____ _____ ml/hr

1-hour limit (mg): _____ (max/hr _____ mg)

If pain still is not controlled after 1 hour, increase PCA dose

by _____ mg, i.e.,_____ ml ONE TIME ONLY.

If pain still is not controlled after 1 additional hour, reduce

lockout interval by _____ minutes ONE TIME ONLY.

No systemic or oral analgesics to be given except by order of the Pain Service Department.

MONITORING: Refer to Pain Control Flow Sheet/Medication Administration Record

_____ M.D.

Fig. 3.3 A sample of the prescription form used at Lincoln Medical and Mental Health Center, Bronx, New York.

Table 3.6   Compatibility of Opioid Solutions with Commonly Used Antibiotics

Drug	Morphine	Meperidine
Amikacin	C	C
Ampicillin	C	C
Carbenicillin	C	C
Cefamandole	C	C
Cefazolin	C	C
Cefoperazone	C	I
Ceforanide	C	C
Cefotaxime	C	C
Cefoxitin	C	C
Ceftizoxime	C	C
Cefuroxime	C	C
Cephalothin	C	C
Cephapirin	C	C
Chloramphenicol	C	C
Clindamycin	C	C
Doxycycline	C	C
Erythromycin	C	C
Gentamicin	C	C
Kanamycin	C	C
Metronidazole	C	C
Mezlocillin	C	I
Minocycline	I	I
Moxalactam	C	C
Nafcillin	C	I
Oxacillin	C	C
Penicillin G benzathine	C	C
Penicillin G potassium	C	C
Penicillin G procaine	C	C
Piperacillin	C	C
Tetracycline	I	I
Ticarcillin	C	C
Tobramycin	C	C
Trimethoprim sulfate	C	C
Vancomycin	C	C

C = compatible with the drugs used in PCA devices; I = incompatible with the drugs used in PCA devices.
Source: AL Nieves-Cordero, HM Luciw, BF Souney. Compatibility of narcotic analgesic solutions with various antibiotics during simulated y-site injections. Am J Hosp Pharm 1985;42:1108.

REFERENCES

1. Hull CJ, Sibbald A. Control of postoperative pain by interactive demand analgesia. Br J Anaesth 1981;53:385.
2. Hull CJ. Apparatus: An On-Demand Analgesia Computer (ODAC). In M Harmer, M Rosen, MD Vickers (eds), Patient-Controlled Analgesia. Oxford: Blackwell, 1985;83.
3. Evans JM, McCarthy JP, Rosen M, et al. Apparatus for patient controlled administration of intravenous narcotics during labour. Lancet 1976;1:17.
4. McKenna TR, Branigan TA, Sorocki AH. Pharmacy-initiated introduction of patient-controlled analgesia to a 400-bed community hospital. Am J Hosp Pharm 1989;46:291.
5. Baumann TJ, Batenhorst RL, Graves DA, et al. Patient-controlled analgesia in the terminally ill cancer patient. Drug Intel Clin Pharm 1986;20:297.
6. McAllister JC. The Painless Path to PCA: An Approach for Success—Development of a Pain Management Program [monograph]. North Chicago: Abbott Laboratories, 1988.

SUGGESTED READING

Ferrante FM, Ostheimer GW, Covino BG. Patient-Controlled Analgesia. Oxford: Blackwell, 1990.

Heath ML, Thomas VJ. Patient-Controlled Analgesia: Confidence in Postoperative Pain Control. Oxford: Oxford Medical Publications, 1993.

Harmer M, Rosen M, Vickers MD. Patient-Controlled Analgesia. Oxford: Blackwell, 1985.

4

Patient Selection and Education

Although PCA was initially described for the treatment of acute pain in the postoperative period, its principle has been applied to several other areas of pain management. Table 4.1 lists clinical circumstances in which appropriate forms of PCA are indicated for pain control.

CONTRAINDICATIONS FOR PCA

There are few absolute contraindications to the use of PCA. Generally, PCA is contraindicated in individuals unable or unwilling to comprehend or activate the PCA device [1]. Children younger than 6–7 years of age, as well as individuals with active psychiatric disease, organic brain syndrome, or dementia, are examples of patients who are unlikely to benefit from PCA. An allergy to PCA medication is another absolute contraindication. History of drug abuse does not preclude the use of PCA. In fact, with appropriate pump settings that take into consideration the patient's opioid tolerance, PCA may provide superior pain relief and reduce confrontations and conflicts frequently present during conventional IM analgesia in patients with a history of drug abuse. Opioid techniques should be avoided in patients with increased intracranial pressure, as well as in morbidly obese patients with obstructive sleep apnea or hypoventilation syndromes [1]. There are also method-specific considerations that contraindicate PCA, such as an abnormal coagulation status or infection

Table 4.1   PCA: Major Clinical Indications

Acute pain
  Postoperative
    Abdominal surgery [21]
    Thoracic surgery [22]
    Orthopedic surgery [23]
    Gynecologic surgery [24]
    Cesarean section [25]
    Urologic surgery [26]
    Head and neck surgery [27]
  Labor and delivery [28]
  Pediatrics [2]
  Trauma [29]
  Sickle-cell disease [30]
Chronic pain
  Cancer [31]

Table 4.2   PCA: Absolute Contraindications

Inability and/or unwillingness to understand the concept of PCA
Inability and/or unwillingness to activate the PCA device
Allergy to PCA medication
Abnormal coagulation status (epidural PCA)
Infection at an insertion site (epidural PCA)

at the insertion site of an epidural catheter. Table 4.2 outlines the
general contraindications to PCA therapy.

CLINICAL USES OF PCA

PCA is now a well-established method of pain control in pediatric
and adolescent patients. The safety and efficacy of IV, epidural,
transnasal, subcutaneous, inhalational, and oral forms of PCA in the
pediatric population have been described in numerous clinical situations, including burn injury and sickle-cell disease [2, 3–12]. Primar-

ily, PCA has been used for postoperative pain control following major abdominal, thoracic, and orthopedic surgery as well as for short orthopedic procedures in emergency departments [8, 9, 12, 13]. Both types of IV PCA—on-demand dosing with and without background infusion—have been successfully used in children recovering from lower abdominal surgery [2, 3]. As in adults, the background infusion has not been shown to improve pain scores or patient satisfaction [2, 3]. Better sleep patterns were noted, however, with background infusion [2, 3]. Children undergoing a bone marrow transplant have been safely managed in the postoperative period with IV PCA with and without background infusion [14].

PCA IN CHILDREN

Although a PCA technique is not suitable for patients younger than 6–7 years of age, an occasional intelligent and motivated 5-year-old patient may be able to use it effectively [15]. Regardless of age, the child should be able to recognize different intensities of pain and operate the PCA device [15]. Children with developmental delay and cerebral palsy are not suitable candidates for PCA [15]. Preoperative education of parents and children is of utmost importance if pediatric PCA is to be successful [15].

Parent-Controlled Analgesia

Parent-controlled analgesia has been used for younger children [16]. Following appropriate screening, parents are trained to assess the intensity of children's pain and sedation and then are allowed to administer the analgesic from the PCA infuser [16]. This technique is useful in children who require long-term outpatient IV opioids for pain control [16].

Nurse-Controlled Analgesia

Nurse-controlled analgesia has been evaluated for pediatric patients unable to use conventional PCA in an intensive care unit [17]. It has been found to be a safe and efficient modality of analgesic administration. However, nurses have been shown to consistently underestimate the pain level of their patients [17].

PCA AND DRUG ABUSE

As mentioned earlier, patients with acute pain and a positive history of drug abuse can be appropriate candidates for PCA. Such patients may be commonly classified into three groups: (1) patients who currently abuse opioids, (2) patients who no longer abuse opioids, and (3) patients in methadone maintenance programs [18]. All three groups should be presumed to have a significant degree of pharmacologic tolerance to opioids that will usually dictate the suitable adjustments of PCA prescription to accommodate the need for higher doses and shorter intervals, because tolerance to opioid analgesics decreases the duration of effective analgesia [19]. In addition, patients actively abusing illegal drugs, such as heroin or cocaine, may have coincidental psychiatric disturbances (e.g., anxiety or depression) that affect pain perception. Proper treatment should be considered for those conditions. Opioid analgesia should not be replaced with nonopioid drugs in active addicts. On the contrary, patients who no longer abuse opioids may benefit from nonopioid or regional pain management techniques, if applicable clinically; some of them may become quite uncomfortable about the prospect of opioid administration. Patients on methadone maintenance may be given IV methadone PCA for pain control. The opioid agonist-antagonists are absolutely contraindicated in any patient with a known or suspected history of drug addiction. These medications may cause dangerous withdrawal symptoms and are inappropriate for severe pain because of their ceiling effect.

Management of PCA in drug-addicted patients with acute pain should take into consideration pharmacologic tolerance and the possibility of inadequate PCA dosing, concomitant psychological disorders and their treatment, the inability of patients to limit their drug-seeking behavior, and the potential for tampering with PCA equipment by patients and their family or friends.

PATIENT EDUCATION

Patient education about PCA should begin as early in the preoperative period as possible. Preferably, the initial information should be given to the patient during the preadmission visit or, at the latest, during the preanesthetic evaluation. In addition to explaining the basic principles of PCA, patients ideally should be shown the device that they will use postoperatively [20]. They should also be encouraged to activate the system and become familiar with the alarm sounds and lights of a device. It is good practice to involve a close relative, if possible, in the education process, especially if the patient is a child. Relatives should be strictly forbidden to administer the medication for the patient, however, unless they are part of parent-controlled analgesia. In addition to verbal information, patients should be provided with written information in the form of leaflets or brochures (Table 4.3). Information materials should use a simple language and contain diagrams. These brochures may be provided by the surgeon's office or sent out from the admission office. Translations should be available for patients with limited English language skills.

The education process should allow patients to ask questions and express their doubts. Sufficient time should be devoted to addressing patients' concerns and clarifying any misinterpretations. Information leaflets can be written in a question-and-answer format and contain the most frequently asked questions with explanations. It has been shown that some patients may not completely understand the concept or the particular details of PCA even with an exceptionally full explanation [20]. Therefore, it is very important to implement review and observation procedures that will detect misunderstandings and misinformation.

Table 4.3   Intravenous PCA: Patient Information Leaflet

Painless Medical Center—Acute Pain Service

Patient Information for Patient-Controlled Analgesia

You will not feel pain during the surgery because your anesthesia care provider will give you anesthetics and other pain-relieving medications. Most operations, however, are associated with some degree of pain after surgery. We offer a safe and effective method of pain relief called *patient-controlled analgesia* (PCA).

Q.   What is PCA?

A.   PCA is a modern technique of pain relief. As the name indicates, you (the patient) decide when and how much pain-relieving medicine you will receive.

Q.   Does it mean that I will give myself "shots"?

A.   No. The PCA system consists of an infusing device or "pump" that will give you prescribed dose of medicine whenever you press the button. There is no need to call the nurse for a painkiller. Better yet, you will not feel the "shot" because the pump infuses the medicine directly into your existing intravenous (IV) line. So no more needles. You will start feeling the effect of the medicine in a few minutes.

Q.   What if I give myself too much medicine? Or too little?

A.   The PCA pump is programmed by the nurse according to the prescription given to you by your anesthesiologist. The prescription includes a so-called lockout period, which is the time period when you will not be able to receive any medication. The lockout period prevents you from giving yourself too much medicine. In addition, the nurse will check your condition periodically, and if you still have some pain, the dose of medicine will be increased.

Q.   The pump is making strange noises. Why?

A.   The PCA infuser will sound a beep each time it gives you medication. A different sound means that the pump may be empty or the IV line is occluded. Call the nurse if the noise persists or you do not feel pain relief after injection.

Q.   When should I press the button?

A.   You should press the button when you start feeling the pain. DO NOT wait until you have a lot of pain! You should also give yourself medication before painful activities such as getting out of bed or coughing.

Q. Does PCA have any side effects?
A. Occasionally the PCA medicine may make you nauseous. Just inform the nurse and you will be given appropriate treatment. You may also feel drowsy after several injections.
Q. Where can I get more information about PCA?
A. Before your surgery you can ask your anesthesiologist about the details of the PCA infuser or other PCA-related questions.

REFERENCES

1. Smythe M. Patient-controlled analgesia: a review. Pharmacotherapy 1992;12:132.
2. Doyle E, Robinson D, Morton NS. Comparison of patient-controlled analgesia with and without a background infusion after lower abdominal surgery in children. Br J Anaesth 1993;71:670.
3. Doyle E, Harper I, Morton NS. Patient-controlled analgesia with low dose background infusions after lower abdominal surgery in children. Br J Anaesth 1993;71:818.
4. Caudle CL, Freid EB, Bailey AG, et al. Epidural fentanyl infusion with patient-controlled epidural analgesia for postoperative analgesia in children. J Pediatr Surg 1993;28:554.
5. Goodarzi M, Shier NH, Ogden JA. Epidural versus patient-controlled analgesia with morphine for postoperative pain after orthopaedic procedures in children. J Pediatr Orthop 1993;13:663.
6. Tobias JD, Rasmussen GE. Transnasal butorphanol for postoperative analgesia following paediatric surgery in a third world country. Paediatr Anaesth 1995;5:63.
7. Doyle E, Morton NS, McNicol LR. Comparison of patient-controlled analgesia in children by i.v. and s.c. routes of administration. Br J Anaesth 1994;72:533.
8. Hennrikus WL, Simpson RB, Klingelberger CE, Reis MT. Self-administered nitrous oxide analgesia for pediatric fracture reductions. J Pediatr Orthop 1994;14:538.
9. Hennrikus WL, Shin AY, Klingelberger CE. Self-administered nitrous oxide and a hematoma block for analgesia in the outpatient reduction of fractures in children. J Bone Joint Surg Am 1995;77:335.

10. Litman RS, Shapiro BS. Oral patient-controlled analgesia in adolescents. J Pain Symptom Manage 1992;7:78.

11. Gaukroger PB, Chapman MJ, Davey RB. Pain control in paediatric burns—the use of patient-controlled analgesia. Burns 1991;17:396.

12. Rodgers BM, Webb CJ, Stergios D, Newman BM. Patient-controlled analgesia in pediatric surgery. J Pediatr Surg 1988;23:259.

13. Berde CB, Lehn BM, Yee JD, et al. Patient-controlled analgesia in children and adolescents: a randomized, prospective comparison with intramuscular administration of morphine for postoperative analgesia. J Pediatr 1991;118:460.

14. Dunbar PJ, Buckley P, Gavrin JR, et al. Use of patient-controlled analgesia for pain control for children receiving bone marrow transplant. J Pain Symptom Manage 1995;10:604.

15. Wilder RT, Berde CB. Acute Pain in Children. In PP Raj (ed), Current Review of Pain. Philadelphia: Current Medicine, 1994;93.

16. Broadman LM. Patient-Controlled Analgesia in Children and Adolescents. In FM Ferrante, GW Ostheimer, BG Covino (eds), Patient-Controlled Analgesia. Boston: Blackwell, 1990;129.

17. Weldon BC, Connor M, White PF. Pediatric PCA: the role of concurrent opioid infusions and nurse-controlled analgesia. Clin J Pain 1993;9:26.

18. Fultz JM, Sonay EC. Guidelines for the management of hospitalized narcotic addicts. Ann Intern Med 1975;82:815.

19. Houde RW. The Use and Misuse of Narcotics in the Treatment of Chronic Pain. In JJ Bonica (ed), International Symposium on Pain (vol 4). Advances in Neurology. New York: Raven, 1974;527.

20. Heath ML, Thomas VJ. Patient-controlled analgesia. Confidence in postoperative pain control. Oxford: Oxford University Press, 1993;55.

21. Albert JM, Talbot TM. Patient-controlled analgesia vs. conventional intramuscular analgesia following colon surgery. Dis Colon Rectum 1988;31(2):83.

22. Boulanger A, Choiniere M, Roy D, et al. Comparison between patient-controlled analgesia and intramuscular meperidine after thoracotomy. Can J Anaesth 1993;40:409.

23. Scalley RD, Berquist KD, Cochran RS. Patient-controlled analgesia in orthopedic procedures. Orthop Rev 1988;17:1106.

24. Ginsberg B, Gil KM, Muir M, et al. The influence of lockout intervals and drug selection on patient-controlled analgesia following gynecological surgery. Pain 1995;62:95.

25. Parker RK, White PF. Epidural patient-controlled analgesia: an alternative to intravenous patient-controlled analgesia for pain relief after cesarean delivery. Anesth Analg 1992;75:245.

26. See WA, Fuller JR, Toner ML. An outcome study of patient-controlled morphine analgesia, with or without ketorolac, following radical retropubic prostatectomy. J Urol 1995;154:1429.

27. Cannon CR. Patient-controlled analgesia (PCA) in head and neck surgery. Otolaryngol Head Neck Surg 1990;103:748.

28. Ferrante FM, Rosinia FA, Gordon C, Datta S. The role of continuous background infusions in patient-controlled epidural analgesia for labor and delivery. Anesth Analg 1994;79:80.

29. Hauer M, Cram E, Titler M, et al. Intravenous patient-controlled analgesia in critically ill postoperative/trauma patients: research-based practice recommendations. Dimens Crit Care Nurs 1995;14:144.

30. Shapiro BS, Cohen DE, Howe CJ. Patient-controlled analgesia for sickle-cell–related pain. J Pain Symptom Manage 1993;8:22.

31. Citron ML, Kalra JM, Seltzer VL, et al. Patient-controlled analgesia for cancer pain: a long-term study of inpatient and outpatient use. Cancer Invest 1992;10:335.

5

Nursing Care and Monitoring

NURSING CARE

Because PCA and patient-controlled epidural analgesia involve the use of opioids and local anesthetics, the role of nurses in monitoring patients for adequate pain control and prevention of adverse outcome is vital. Nursing involvement starts in the preoperative period and extends up to the discharge of the patient. The nursing staff should be involved in the development of policies and educational programs for the hospital staff. Important concerns to be discussed in the policy are shown in Table 5.1. The educational program should include practical training so that nurses are comfortable using the device as well as teaching its use to patients [1]. Once in use, PCA is superior to the standard IM or IV regimes (Table 5.2 and Figure 5.1).

In conjunction with the anesthesiologist and surgeon, patient selection for PCA can be made by the nursing staff. Patients requiring PCA should be explained its purpose and use by the nursing staff before surgery. The nursing staff should provide the patient with printed information with or without an instructional videotape. Patients who are scheduled for same-day admission can be given this information at the preadmission testing clinic. The anxiety of patients regarding postoperative pain control can be decreased by making them feel that they will actively participate in their pain management and improve its therapeutic effectiveness [2].

Table 5.1   Policy Issues for PCA

Information about equipment (e.g., manufacturer)
How to set up the equipment
How to operate the equipment
Modes of dosing
Where to get the medication
Where to get tubing, syringes, or cartridges
What information should be obtained from the postanesthesia care
    unit nurse
When to stop PCA
How to respond to alarms
Troubleshooting
Monitoring protocols
Documentation
How to respond to side effects
What to do and who to call in an emergency
What should be available in an emergency

Table 5.2   Advantages of PCA

Improved pain control
Decreased nursing time
Increased nursing time for other patient care
More effective and decreased drug consumption
Greater patient satisfaction
Greater patient independence
Fewer complications
Rapid recovery and early discharge
Lower health costs
Early availability of beds for needy patients

   Nurse interviews also act as an initial screening procedure for
uncovering any contraindications for the use of PCA (e.g., mental
impairment or severe chronic obstructive pulmonary disease) [3, 4].
For example, a patient who experiences severe nausea, vomiting,

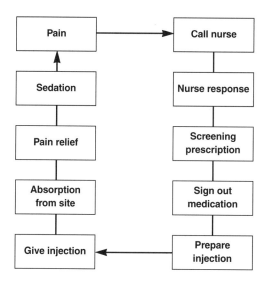

Fig. 5.1 Conventional IM pain relief delay cycle.

and/or pruritus from narcotics may benefit from antiemetic (e.g., metoclopramide) or antipruritic (e.g., diphenhydramine) therapy.

Postanesthesia care unit (PACU) nurses should be informed of the need for a PCA device before transfer of the patient from the operating room so they can prepare the PCA device. Because the PACU observation includes frequent monitoring of vital signs, respiratory rate, and pulse oximetry, initiation of PCA does not require any additional monitoring other than recording pain scores. Every PCA patient should be brought to a comfortable state in the recovery room. The time spent in the recovery room should be used to assess any side effects and initiate the monitoring of PCA. The moni-

Table 5.3   Questions for the Recovery Room Nurse from the Ward Nurse (When Receiving a Patient Using PCA)

What is the diagnosis of the patient?
What procedure was performed?
What medication is the patient receiving?
What is the prescription for PCA?
Is the patient receiving a basal rate?
Is the patient comfortable?
Did the patient experience any side effects?
What is the prescription for side effects?
Does the pump have enough medicine?
Has the patient activated the PCA device?
Who should be called in case of emergency?
What is the weight of the patient?
Does the patient have a history of drug abuse?

toring form should include records of standard vital signs, continuous infusion rate, number of attempts by patient to administer analgesia, pain scores, and frequent side effects, including sedation scores. The commonly used pain scoring scale is a 0–10 scale that can also be printed on the monitoring form.

Once patients have adequately recovered from anesthesia, they should be transferred to the regular ward. Before disconnecting the PCA device from the electrical source, the monitoring form should be updated from the PCA device if the device is equipped with memory function. When receiving the patient in the ward, nurses should ask the questions provided by the PACU nurse (Table 5.3). Ward nurses should also assess the patient frequently in the early phases for adequate pain control, stability of vital signs, and side effects. Once the patient is comfortable, the level of monitoring can be reduced.

Nurses can play an important role in the successful implementation of PCA. They can also give important feedback about various difficulties encountered with PCA devices. Regular bedside assess-

Table 5.4   Side Effects Associated with PCA and Opioid Use

Nausea and vomiting
Pruritus
Urinary retention
Constipation
Excessive sweating and pallor
Inadequate pain control
IV-site infiltration
IV-site infection
Sedation
Euphoria
Respiratory depression
Hypotension
Ileus

ments of patients and proper use of accumulated information can minimize the complications and improve patient satisfaction.

MONITORING

Adequate monitoring of patients on PCA can prevent side effects and result in a satisfied patient with adequate pain control. Monitoring should include frequent checks for adequacy of analgesia. Newer devices have the capability of retrieving hourly data from the pump memory. By checking the number of attempts made by the patient and the amount of drug delivered, the physician can adjust the dose prescription to achieve maximum benefits. Anticipatory dosing in the ward at the time of mobility and dressing changes can be beneficial and should be encouraged with input from the nursing staff to achieve maximum benefits.

A standard protocol of minor and major side effects to be monitored (Table 5.4) along with the monitoring of pain scores should be made.

Table 5.5   Factors Associated with an Increased Risk of Nausea and Vomiting

Prolonged starvation
Hypoxia
Hypovolemia
Hypotension
Gynecologic surgery
Laparoscopic surgery
Middle ear surgery
Type of anesthetic agent
Previous history of nausea and vomiting
Pain
Female gender

Nausea and Vomiting

The incidence of nausea and vomiting varies from 10% to 20% in patients receiving PCA [5]. Various factors play a role in postoperative nausea and vomiting. The use of PCA has been shown to decrease the incidence of nausea and vomiting [6]. The mechanism of opioid-induced nausea and vomiting is via stimulation of chemoreceptor trigger zones in the brain stem. The route of administration does not influence the incidence of nausea and vomiting [7, 8]. Factors that can increase nausea and vomiting are listed in Table 5.5. The total amount of opioid administered has shown no consistent relationship with incidence of nausea and vomiting [9]. The treatment of nausea and vomiting includes avoiding factors such as prolonged starvation, hypoxemia, and hypotension. Intractable nausea and vomiting should be treated with agents such as prochlorperazine, droperidol, metoclopramide, or ondansetron. Treatment guidelines for nausea and vomiting are shown in Figure 5.2.

Pruritus

Pruritus is associated with all modes of opioid administration. The exact etiology is unknown but pruritus associated with morphine and

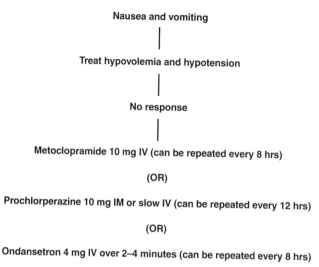

Nausea and vomiting

|

Treat hypovolemia and hypotension

|

No response

|

Metoclopramide 10 mg IV (can be repeated every 8 hrs)

(OR)

Prochlorperazine 10 mg IM or slow IV (can be repeated every 12 hrs)

(OR)

Ondansetron 4 mg IV over 2–4 minutes (can be repeated every 8 hrs)

Fig. 5.2 Treatment guidelines for nausea and vomiting in the postanesthesia care unit or ward.

meperidine may be attributed to histamine release. The incidence and severity of pruritus depends on the route of administration and varies considerably. The frequency of pruritus varies in this order: intrathecal > epidural > IV > PCA > IM [7, 8, 10, 11]. It should be treated with diphenhydramine (Benadryl), 25 mg IM (can be repeated every 6 hours) [7]. If there is no response to diphenhydramine, the opioid antagonist naloxone in incremental doses of 0.01 mg IM should be given. Figure 5.3 outlines guidelines for the treatment of pruritus. Prophylactic naloxone infusions have been suggested to prevent pruritus [12].

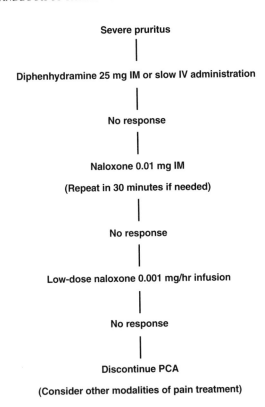

Fig. 5.3   Treatment guidelines for pruritus.

Table 5.6   Factors Associated with Increased Risk of Respiratory Depression

Pre-existing medical diseases (e.g., chronic obstructive pulmonary
    disease, sleep apnea syndrome, obesity)
Immediate postoperative period
Residual effect of anesthetic agents
Upper abdominal or thoracic surgery
Ventilation and perfusion abnormalities
Hypotension and hypovolemia
Hypoxemia
Hypercarbia
Aspiration
Continuous opioid infusion
Epidural or intrathecal opioids
Infiltrated IV site acting as a depot

Urinary Retention

Urinary retention is common after surgery. Addition of opioids, especially intrathecally and epidurally, may add to the problem. Most patients receiving epidural opioids may already have a urinary catheter in place. Urinary retention should be treated with bladder catheterization to prevent the discomfort of distention. Patients may rarely require naloxone to reverse the opioid effects.

Respiratory Depression

Opioids administered via any PCA device have a risk of respiratory depression. Continuous infusions are associated with an increased risk [13, 14]. Factors associated with increased risk of respiratory depression along with prevention and emergency treatment guidelines are listed in Tables 5.6 and 5.7.

Judicious selection of patients for PCA and adequate monitoring can prevent complications. The use of PCA is associated with decreased opioid use and usually decreased complications.

Table 5.7   Guidelines for the Prevention and Treatment of Respiratory Depression

Avoid continuous infusion in the ward
Carefully select patients for opioid PCA
Use other modalities of pain relief, such as infiltration of epidural local
   anesthetics in patients with severe respiratory disease
Monitor the patient for obstructed airway
Monitor sedation level
Use pulse oximetry in patients with increased risk of respiratory
   depression
Give supplemental oxygen if needed
Monitor apneic episodes
Check the color of patient frequently
Keep intubation and resuscitation equipment available in the immediate
   vicinity
Maintain easy availability of opioid antagonist
Follow these steps in case of emergency:
   Stop PCA
   Call for help
   Maintain airway
   Give IV naloxone, 0.1 mg, and repeat if necessary
   Start IV infusion if required
   Intubate the patient if needed
   Maintain and monitor vital signs
   Look for other causes

REFERENCES

1. Kane NE, Lehman ME, Dugger R, et al. Patient-controlled analgesia: a review of the current state of knowledge. Semin Anesth 1986;5:100.
2. Paice JA. New delivery systems in pain management. Nurse Clin North Am 1987;22:715.
3. Barkas G, Duafala M. Advances in cancer pain management: a review of patient-controlled analgesia. J Pain Symptom Manage 1988;3:150.
4. Fitzgerald JJ, Shamy PG. Let your patient control his analgesia. Nursing 1987;17:48.

5. Bahar M, Rosen M, Vickers MD. Self-administered nalbuphine, morphine and pethidine. Comparison, by intravenous route, following cholecystectomy. Anesthesia 1985;40:529.

6. Bollish SJ, Collins CL, Kirking DM, et al. Efficacy of patient-controlled versus conventional analgesia for postoperative pain. Clin Pharm 1985;4:48.

7. Daley DM, Sandler AN, Turner KE, et al. A comparison of epidural and intramuscular morphine in patients following cesarean section. Anesthesiology 1990;72:289.

8. Eisenach JC, Grice SC, Dewan DM. Patient-controlled analgesia following cesarean section: a comparison with epidural and intramuscular narcotics. Anesthesiology 1988;68:444.

9. Owen H, Plummer JL, Armstrong LE, et al. Variables in patient-controlled analgesia: 1. Bolus size. Anesthesia 1989;44:7.

10. Harrison DM, Sinatra R, Morgese L, et al. Epidural narcotic and patient-controlled analgesia for post–cesarean section pain relief. Anesthesiology 1988;68:454.

11. Loper KA, Ready LB. Epidural morphine after anterior cruciate ligament repair: a comparison with patient-controlled intravenous morphine following cholecystectomy. Anesth Analg 1989;68:350.

12. Gowan JD, Hurtig JB, Fraser RA, et al. Naloxone infusion after prophylactic epidural morphine: effects on incidence of postoperative side effects and quality of analgesia. Can J Anaesth 1988;35:143.

13. Catley DM, Thornton C, Jordan C, et al. Postoperative respiratory depression associated with continuous morphine infusion [abstract]. Br J Anaesth 1982;281:478.

14. Catling JA, Pinto DM, Jordan C, et al. Respiratory effects of analgesia after cholecystectomy: comparison of continuous and intermittent papaveretum. Br J Med 1980;281:478.

6

Complications of Patient-Controlled Analgesia

PCA is considered a safe method of pain control. The initial apprehension and skepticism of the medical community toward PCA have been replaced by a prevailing acceptance and awareness of the advantages and benefits of PCA to patients, professional staff, and hospitals [1]. The partial explanation of this change of attitude probably lies in the exceptionally positive safety profile of PCA. PCA complications are rare and easily recognized and can be managed with proper training and monitoring. In general, the problems associated with PCA can be classified into three groups:

1. Medication related
2. Equipment related
3. Patient related

MEDICATION-RELATED COMPLICATIONS

Medication-related complications are essentially the side effects of opioids, but rare instances of drug interactions should not be overlooked. The adverse effects of opioids are summarized in Table 6.1 and have already been partly discussed in Chapter 5.

Respiratory Depression

Respiratory depression is the most dangerous complication of opioid PCA. It is a rare, dose-dependent phenomenon and a potentially fatal complication. The mechanism of respiratory depression

Table 6.1   Side Effects of Opioids

Respiratory depression
Sedation
Nausea and vomiting
Ileus
Urinary retention
Pruritus

Table 6.2   PCA: Risk Factors for Respiratory Depression

Background infusion
Advanced age
Sedative/hypnotic interactions
Sleep apnea syndrome

involves a reduction in the response of the brain stem respiratory center to increases in carbon dioxide tension and is usually preceded by excessive drowsiness and decreased respiratory rate. Respiratory depression is most likely to occur after an accidental overdose caused by a technical problem (e.g., infuser or syringe failure), human error (e.g., incorrect programming), or injection by someone other than the patient [2–5]. It has been suggested that patients receiving intravenous (IV) PCA with background infusion are more likely to develop respiratory depression [2, 4–8]. Other factors associated with the increased risk of respiratory depression include advanced age, administration of sedative/hypnotic medications, and pre-existing sleep apnea syndrome (Table 6.2) [7].

The incidence of serious respiratory-related critical events was 0.1% in one report of 3,785 patients receiving PCA therapy [4]. The risk of respiratory depression during PCA therapy can be reduced by avoiding background infusion and using cautious dose and interval settings for elderly PCA patients and PCA patients with sleep

Table 6.3   PCA: Risk Factors for Nausea and Vomiting

Younger age
Female gender (especially in immediate premenstrual period)
Lack of preoperative adverse medical conditions
Elective procedures
Nonsmoking
Longer duration of anesthesia
Inhaled anesthetics (nitrous oxide)
Opioid premedication
Intraoperative opioids
Gynecologic; ophthalmologic; and ear, nose, and throat surgery
Laparoscopy, arthroscopy, strabismus repair

apnea syndrome. Treatment of respiratory depression ranges from discontinuing PCA to full-blown management of respiratory arrest using positive pressure ventilation, intubation, and increasing doses of IV naloxone.

Nausea and Vomiting

Nausea and vomiting occur in 10–20% of patients receiving opioid PCA [1]. These complications continue to be described as some of the most undesirable patient experiences associated with PCA [9]. Postoperative nausea and vomiting remain poorly understood, but several risk factors that predispose patients to their development have been identified (Table 6.3) [10].

Traditional treatment of PCA-induced nausea and vomiting includes IV droperidol, metoclopramide, or prochlorperazine. Drowsiness and extrapyramidal symptoms are principal side effects of these medications. There has been recent interest in combining antiemetics with analgesics in every PCA dose [11–13]. In general, this approach reduces the incidence (droperidol) and severity (metoclopramide) of nausea and vomiting associated with PCA [11–13]; however, the addition of droperidol to the PCA solution results in higher sedation and drowsiness scores [11, 12]. Propofol administered in subhypnotic doses (e.g., 10-mg bolus) or as a low-dose infusion for 24 hours postoperatively has not been shown to be more effective in prevention or treatment of nausea and vomiting than droperidol, metoclopramide, or intralipid infusion [10, 14]. Ondansetron has emerged as a useful treatment for PCA-induced nausea and vomiting [15]. It has been demonstrated that ondansetron is more effective than droperidol in decreasing the frequency and severity of PCA-related nausea and vomiting without producing untoward sedation [15]. The most recent investigations of PCA-induced nausea and vomiting focus on the effectiveness of combining droperidol and ondansetron for prevention. Clearly, such a combination has been proven superior to either drug used alone for prophylaxis of nausea and vomiting associated with PCA [16, 17].

Ileus and Urinary Retention

Prolonged ileus and urinary retention are well-known side effects of opioids. Administration of IV PCA has been associated with both complications, but incidence depends on surgical techniques and procedures [18–23]. One study reported a decrease in length of postoperative ileus in patients receiving epidural infusion of bupivacaine and morphine [24].

Pruritus

Pruritus is a distressing complication, especially after epidural or intrathecal administration of opioids. The incidence and severity of pruritus are less prevalent with IV and intramuscular opioids. Pruritus that develops after administration of IV opioids is usually responsive to antihistamines such as diphenhydramine or hydroxyzine. On the other hand, pruritus seen after intrathecal or epidural opioids is frequently unresponsive to antihistamines and may require small doses of naloxone, naltrexone, or nalbuphine [25].

Drug Interactions

The potential for drug interactions is an important consideration in prescribing and administering PCA. Central nervous system depressant effects of opioids are potentiated by sedatives, antihistamines, phenothiazines, butyrophenones, monoamine oxidase (MAO) inhibitors, and tricyclic antidepressants [26]. It is especially critical to remember the toxic and fatal interaction between meperidine and MAO inhibitors, which may result in hyperthermia, hypertension, and seizures. It is also worth remembering that alpha$_2$-agonists such as clonidine enhance opioid analgesia [26]. Local anesthetic (lidocaine and bupivacaine) interactions that are pertinent during PCA administration include reduction of clearance with concomitant administration of beta-blocking medications and cimetidine [26].

EQUIPMENT-RELATED COMPLICATIONS

Equipment-related complications can lead to inadequate analgesia or overdose. The most common cause of equipment-related overdose is initial incorrect programming of the device [1]. Mechanical problems associated with PCA infusers include cracked drug vials or syringes, defective one-way valves, a broken lock, and a defective alarm system [27]. Early PCA systems were vulnerable to a continuous infusion of opioids after accidental damage to drug vials or syringes, the so-called siphon effect [1]. This problem has been corrected by installing antisiphon valves. Inadvertent infiltration or clamping of the PCA tubing or main IV line results in inadequate analgesia.

It is preferable to establish separate IV access for PCA administration. Opioid solution should be connected to the main line as close to an IV cannula as possible to prevent accumulation of several doses in the extension tubing and subsequent delivery of large boluses of opioid. In addition, the PCA tubing should contain an antireflux valve that blocks retrograde flow of fluids into the infuser [28].

PATIENT-RELATED COMPLICATIONS

Patient-related complications are usually the result of elaborate efforts of drug-abusing patients to bypass the security features of PCA devices. Forms of tampering with the PCA infusers may include mechanical damage to a locking mechanism, aspiration of opioids from extension tubing, and memorizing access codes to reprogram prescriptions. Such behavior is easily detected by monitoring medication use and the patient's condition.

PCA is not a complication-free technique. However, most of the complications can be minimized by adopting and following clear policies and close monitoring.

REFERENCES

1. Callan CM. An Analysis of Complaints and Complications with Patient-Controlled Analgesia. In FM Ferrante, GW Ostheimer, BG Covino (eds), Patient-Controlled Analgesia. Boston: Blackwell, 1990;139.
2. Thomas DW, Owen H. Patient-controlled analgesia—the need for caution. A case report and review of adverse incidents. Anaesthesia 1988;43:770.
3. Grover ER, Heath ML. Patient-controlled analgesia. A serious incident. Anaesthesia 1992;47:402.
4. Ashburn MA, Love G, Pace NL. Respiratory-related critical events with intravenous patient-controlled analgesia. Clin J Pain 1994;10(1):52.
5. Looi Lyons LC, Chung FF, Chan VW, McQuestion M. Respiratory depression: an adverse outcome during patient controlled analgesia therapy. J Clin Anesth 1996;8:151.
6. Heath ML, Thomas VJ. Minimizing Side Effects. In Patient-Controlled Analgesia. Confidence in Postoperative Pain Control. Oxford: Oxford University Press, 1993;156.
7. Etches RC. Respiratory depression associated with patient-controlled analgesia: a review of eight cases. Can J Anaesth 1994;41:125.
8. Fleming BM, Coombs DW. A survey of complications documented in a quality-control analysis of patient-controlled analgesia in the postoperative patient. J Pain Symptom Manage 1992;7:463.

9. Taylor NM, Hall GM, Salmon P. Patients' experiences of patient-controlled analgesia. Anaesthesia 1996;51:525.

10. Frost EAM. Clinical Problem Solving in the Post Anesthesia Care Unit. Annual Refresher Course Lectures (411). Park Ridge, IL: American Society of Anesthesiologists, 1996.

11. Williams OA, Clarke FL, Harris RW, et al. Addition of droperidol to patient-controlled analgesia: effect on nausea and vomiting. Anaesthesia 1993;48:881.

12. Barrow PM, Hughes DG, Redfern N, Urie J. Influence of droperidol on nausea and vomiting during patient-controlled analgesia. Br J Anaesth 1994;72:460.

13. Walder AD, Aitkenhead AR. Antiemetic efficacy of metoclopramide when included in a patient-controlled analgesia infusion. Anaesthesia 1994;49:804.

14. Montgomery JE, Sutherland CJ, Kestin IG, Sneyd JR. Infusions of sub-hypnotic doses of propofol for the prevention of postoperative nausea and vomiting. Anaesthesia 1996;51:554.

15. Alexander R, Lovell AT, Seingry D, Jones RM. Comparison of ondansetron and droperidol in reducing postoperative nausea and vomiting associated with patient-controlled analgesia. Anaesthesia 1995; 50:1086.

16. Wrench IJ, Ward JE, Walder AD, Hobbs GJ. The prevention of postoperative nausea and vomiting using a combination of ondansetron and droperidol. Anaesthesia 1996;51:776.

17. Pueyo FJ, Carrascosa F, Lopez L, et al. Combination of ondansetron and droperidol in the prophylaxis of postoperative nausea and vomiting. Anesth Analg 1996;83:117.

18. Petros JG, Realica R, Ahmad S, et al. Patient-controlled analgesia and prolonged ileus after uncomplicated colectomy. Am J Surg 1995;170:371.

19. Stanley BK, Noble MJ, Gilliland C, et al. Comparison of patient-controlled analgesia versus intramuscular narcotics in resolution of postoperative ileus after radical retropubic prostatectomy. J Urol 1993;150:1434.

20. LaRosa JA, Saywell RM Jr, Zollinger TW, et al. The incidence of adynamic ileus in postcesarean patients. Patient-controlled analgesia versus intramuscular analgesia. J Reprod Med 1993;38:293.

21. Petros JG, Alameddine F, Testa E, et al. Patient-controlled analgesia and postoperative urinary retention after hysterectomy for benign disease. J Am Coll Surg 1994;179:663.

22. Petros JG, Mallen JK, Howe K, et al. Patient-controlled analgesia and postoperative urinary retention after open appendectomy. Surg Gynecol Obstet 1993;177:172.

23. Petros JG, Rimm EB, Robillard RJ. Factors influencing urinary tract retention after elective open cholecystectomy. Surg Gynecol Obstet 1992;174:497.

24. de Leon-Casasola OA, Karabella D, Lema MJ. Bowel function recovery after radical hysterectomies: thoracic epidural bupivacaine-morphine versus intravenous patient-controlled analgesia with morphine: a pilot study. J Clin Anesth 1996;8:87.

25. Etches RC. Complications of Acute Pain Management. In AN Sandler (ed), Current Concepts in Acute Pain Control. Philadelphia: Saunders, 1992;417.

26. Omoigui S. The Anesthesia Drug Handbook. St. Louis: Mosby–Year Book, 1992;17, 102, 110, 134.

27. Smythe M. Patient-controlled analgesia: a review. Pharmacotherapy 1992;12:132.

28. Heath ML, Thomas VJ. Sources of Danger to the Patient. In Patient-Controlled Analgesia. Confidence in Postoperative Pain Control. Oxford: Oxford University Press, 1993;102.

7

Trauma and Patient-Controlled Analgesia

Traumatic injury is one of the most serious health problems in modern society. Initial treatment efforts in a trauma patient should be directed toward resuscitative and diagnostic processes, and acute pain management should be considered early in the stabilization of the patient. Pain can impede the return of normal pulmonary functions, modify stress response to injury, and alter hemodynamic values and cardiovascular function [1]. Pain also produces immobility and thromboembolic complications. It slows down the recovery from injuries and contributes to increased morbidity [1]. Adequate analgesia is associated with fewer complications and improved outcome.

HEAD INJURY

Head injury patients have a continuously evolving picture for the first few minutes to days. Increased intracranial pressure, cerebral hypoxia, and hypertension are major concerns. Adequate cerebral oxygenation is a priority. These patients also have altered levels of consciousness. Opioids are respiratory depressants and may cause hypercarbia, which in turn, may worsen the cerebral injury. Trauma victims who have an element of head injury are not suitable candidates for opioids and PCA. Moreover, these patients may not be conscious enough to operate the device. Most of these patients, however, also have associated injuries, and once the head injury element is defined, the patient can be prescribed PCA to achieve pain control.

CHEST AND ABDOMINAL INJURIES

Patients with chest and abdominal injuries who are in shock or severe distress require immediate medical attention and transport to the nearest hospital for better outcome [2]. Oxygen delivery and cardiorespiratory stabilization are major concerns in these patients. Tension pneumothorax, cardiac tamponade, hemothorax, hemoperitoneum, and injury to major vessels should be identified and treated with urgency. These patients often require emergency surgery, and postoperative analgesia should be planned based on the condition and outcome of the surgery. If the patient is hemodynamically stable and has no significant coagulation abnormalities, epidural catheter placement should be considered at the end of surgery. Segmental epidural analgesia appears to be preferable for post-thoracotomy patients because it increases the specificity of the pain control site and reduces the dose of analgesia needed for adequate pain relief [3, 4]. Epidural analgesia has been shown to require significantly decreased doses of morphine compared to IV PCA [5, 6]. Besides providing superior pain relief, epidural analgesia can partially attenuate the hormonal stress response to injury and even improve ventilatory function.

Various methods for epidural drug administration include the following: (1) intermittent boluses, (2) continuous infusion, and (3) patient-controlled epidural analgesia (PCEA). Administering intermittent boluses of epidural morphine has its disadvantages, for example, variability in duration of analgesia [7, 8] and tachyphylaxis [9]. It also requires higher doses than does continuous infusion and may have increased side effects [7], including delayed respiratory depression.

Continuous infusion offers therapeutic advantages over intermittent boluses. Addition of local anesthetics, such as bupivacaine, 0.125%, to opioids further reduces the total dosage of opioids and the incidence of side effects [10, 11]. Rapid onset of local anesthetic action provides faster relief to the patient. Continuous epidural analgesia is associated with complications, such as intrathecal migration of catheters, epidural hematomas, infection, and respiratory depression.

Table 7.1   Advantages of Epidural PCA Over Continuous Epidural Infusion and IV PCA

Increased efficiency
Higher patient satisfaction
Decreased opioid usage
Decreased risk of respiratory depression
Decreased sedation
Decreased anxiety
Adjustment of medication by patients
Anticipatory dosing can be performed

Table 7.2   Commonly Prescribed Epidural PCA Prescription

Loading dose	2–3 mg
Basal infusion (optional)	0.4 mg/hr (0.02% solution)
Delay	10–15 mins
Dose	0.2 mg
1 hr maximum	1–2 mg

PCEA has been found to be superior and use decreased dosages of opioids compared to continuous epidural infusion (Table 7.1) [5, 6]. Guidelines for using morphine in PCEA are summarized in Table 7.2.

ORTHOPEDIC INJURIES

Patients with orthopedic injuries can benefit from both IV PCA and PCEA. PCEA was found to be as effective as continuous epidural infusion in patients with post-traumatic pelvic reconstruction [12]. This study showed no recorded incidence of hypotension or respiratory depression. The incidence of nausea, vomiting, and pruritus were similar in both groups. IV PCA should be given to patients who are not candidates for PCEA. Contraindications for PCEA include coagulopathy, spinal injury, head injury infection, and patient refusal.

SUMMARY

Although little data are available about the use of PCA in trauma patients, experience with acute postoperative PCA can be extended to trauma victims. Most of the trauma patients undergo some type of surgery, and surgery is also a form of iatrogenic trauma. A major disadvantage of PCA compared with other methods of parenteral opioid administration is that the trauma patient must be alert and oriented enough to use the device. Do not underestimate pain in intubated patients; an intubated patient who is awake and responsive should be offered PCA.

REFERENCES

1. Lewis KS, Whipple JK, Michael KA, et al. Effect of analgesic treatment on the physiological consequences of acute pain. Am J Hosp 1994;51:1539.
2. Ivatury RR, Rohman M. Emergency department thoracotomy for trauma: collective review. Resuscitation 1987;15:23.
3. Lubenow TR, Durrani Z, Ivankovish AD. Evaluation of continuous epidural fentanyl/butorphanol infusion for postoperative pain. Anesthesiology 1990;73:A800.
4. Rosseel PMJ, Van Der Broeck J, Boer EC, et al. Epidural sufentanil for intraoperative and postoperative analgesia in thoracic surgery: a comparative study with intravenous sufentanil. Acta Anaesthesiol Scand 1988;32:193.
5. Rauck R, Knarr D, Denson D, et al. Comparison of the efficacy of epidural morphine given by intermittent injection or continuous infusion for the management of postoperative pain. Anesthesiology 1986;65:A201.
6. Marlowe S, Engstrom R, White PF. Epidural patient-controlled analgesia (PCA): an alternative to continuous epidural infusions. Pain 1989;37:97.
7. Bromage PR, Camporesi E, Chestnut D. Epidural narcotics for postoperative analgesia. Anesth Analg 1989;59:473.

8. Rutler DV, Skewes DG, Morgan M. Extradural opioids for postoperative analgesia. Br J Anaesth 1981;53:915.

9. Scott NB, Mogense T, Bigler D, et al. Continuous thoracic extradural 0.05% bupivacaine with or without morphine: effect on quality of blockade, lung function and the surgical stress response. Br J Anaesth 1989;62:253.

10. Cullen M, Staren E, Ganzouri A, et al. Continuous thoracic epidural analgesia after major abdominal operations: a randomized prospective double-blind study. Surgery 1985;98:718.

11. Fisher R, Lubenow TR, Liceaga A, et al. Comparison of continuous epidural infusion of fentanyl-bupivacaine and morphine-bupivacaine in the management of postoperative pain. Anesth Analg 1988;67:559.

12. Nolan JP, Dow AA, Parr MJ, et al. Patient-controlled epidural analgesia following post-traumatic pelvic reconstruction. A comparison with continuous epidural analgesia. Anesthesia 1992;47:1037.

8

Chronic Pain and Patient-Controlled Analgesia

The treatment of patients in chronic pain involves an understanding of the pathophysiology of pain and tumors. A targeted history and physical examination can help in planning pain treatment for a patient with chronic pain. Inadequately controlled chronic pain interferes with the patient's emotional and psychological well-being. It also alters the patient's attitude toward health and recovery [1]. Chronic pain can be of malignant and nonmalignant origin. Approximately 50% of patients with advanced cancer pathology have pain [2]. This chapter discusses chronic cancer pain and the role of PCA in its management. Important symptoms of cancer patients are listed in Table 8.1.

PATHOPHYSIOLOGY OF CANCER PAIN

Cancer patients may have pain due to various causes (Table 8.2). Mechanisms responsible for cancer pain are not well understood. Three important recognizable areas have been hypothesized in the occurrence of cancer pain, including (1) nociceptive mechanisms, (2) neuropathic mechanisms, and (3) psychological influences.

Nociceptive pain is pain produced by tumor stimulation of nerve pathways and is often related to the extent of the tumor. Inflammation also plays an important role in determining the characteristics of this pain. Nociceptive pain responds well to opioids [3].

Table 8.1   Symptoms of Cancer Patients

Decreased functional capability
Decreased appetite
Decreased pain threshold
Decreased sleep and altered sleep patterns
Sense of helplessness
Increased anxiety and fear
Depression
Altered appearance
Altered interpersonal relationships
Personal distress
Fatigue
Altered taste
Nausea and vomiting
Dyspnea
Weight loss

Table 8.2   Causes of Pain in Cancer Patients

Tumor infiltration of nerve
Metastasis in bony site
Acute postoperative pain
Invasive diagnostic procedures
Therapeutic procedures
Toxicity of chemotherapy and radiation
Infection

Neuropathic pain refers to pain resulting from direct involvement of the peripheral or central nervous system [4, 5]. Dysesthesia, allodynia, hyperpathia, and changes in the receptor field are often associated with neuropathic pain. These complications are generally associated with lesions of bone or other somatic structures. Neuropathic pain responds poorly to opioids [6].

Table 8.3   Important Cancer Pain Syndromes

Bone metastasis
   Direct activation of local bone nociceptors
   Compression of peripheral nerves
   Compression of nerve roots by spine metastasis
   Headache from base of skull metastasis
Spinal cord compression
Plexopathies due to infiltration by metastasis (cervical, brachial, or
      lumbosacral)
Peripheral neuropathies
   Tumor infiltration
   Postsurgical (e.g., postmastectomy pain)
   Chemotherapy induced (vincristine and cisplatin)
   Radiation induced
Acute postherpetic neuralgia (due to reactivation of herpes zoster by
      immunosuppression)
Cranial neuropathies
Myositis
Visceral pain syndromes

Psychological influences are considered in the type of pain that is not explained by an organic lesion. Various important pain syndromes in cancer patients are listed in Table 8.3.

ASSESSMENT AND THERAPEUTIC STRATEGY

A systematic approach is necessary to achieve therapeutic goals. Guidelines for initial assessment that are helpful in diagnosing and planning the treatment of various pain syndromes are listed in Table 8.4. The initial questionnaire should also include a pain assessment scale for future comparison. Once an initial assessment has been made, a treatment plan should be formulated.

The strategy for treating patients with chronic cancer pain should be to achieve immediate pain relief via a multidisciplinary approach. A subjective method of cancer pain quantification has been reliable

Table 8.4   Guidelines for Initial Pain Assessment

Review old records
Detailed history of patient
    Mode of onset
    Location of pain
    Chronicity
    Duration
    Frequency
    Character and intensity
    Associated factors (e.g., precipitating factors, environmental factors)
Detailed physical examination
Psychological assessment
Socioeconomic consideration
Treatment and its response
Other medical conditions
Appropriate diagnostic workup

in verifying the efficacy of the treatment [7, 8]. Guidelines to the therapeutic strategy for a cancer patient are shown in Table 8.5. The goal of treatment should be symptomatic relief and specific treatment of the tumor. Patients should be evaluated at frequent intervals for adequacy of pain control.

Nonsteroidal Anti-Inflammatory Drugs

Nonsteroidal anti-inflammatory drugs (NSAIDs) are used as an initial therapy for mild pain. They decrease the levels of inflammatory mediators of pain by inhibiting the enzyme cyclooxygenase. NSAIDs are only effective in the early phases of cancer pain; as the disease advances, cancer patients require multiple modalities of treatment. Long-term use of NSAIDs is associated with several side effects (Table 8.6) that should be monitored. Commonly used NSAIDs and their dosages are listed in Table 8.7.

Table 8.5   Therapeutic Strategy Guidelines for Treatment of Pain in Cancer Patients

Nonsteroidal anti-inflammatory drugs
Opioids
Neurolytic block
Ablative surgery and neurosurgery
Adjuvant therapy
    Steroids
    Anticonvulsants
    Antidepressants
Relaxation, imagery therapy, biofeedback, and reframing of negative
    thoughts
Patient education
Psychotherapy
Cutaneous stimulation
Transcutaneous electrical nerve stimulation
Physiotherapy
Acupuncture
Antineoplastic treatment
    Chemotherapy
    Radiotherapy
    Surgery

Table 8.6   Side Effects of Nonsteroidal Anti-Inflammatory Drugs

Major
    Renal failure
    Hepatic dysfunction
    Bleeding
    Gastric ulceration
Minor
    Dyspepsia
    Heartburn
    Nausea and vomiting
    Anorexia
    Epigastric pain
    Bloating

Table 8.7   Dosages of Commonly Prescribed, Orally Administered Nonsteroidal Anti-Inflammatory Drugs

Acetaminophen	10–15 mg/kg q4h
Aspirin	10–15 mg/kg q4h
Ibuprofen	10 mg/kg q6–8h
Choline magnesium trisalicylate	25 mg/kg q8h
Diflunisal (Dolobid)	500 mg q12h
Etodolac (Lodine)	200–400 mg q8h
Fenoprofen (Nalfon)	300–600 mg q6h
Ketoprofen (Orudis)	25–60 mg q6–8h
Ketorolac	10 mg q6h
Meclofenamate (Meclomen)	50–10 mg q6h
Mefenamic acid (Ponstel)	250 mg q6h
Naproxen (Naprosyn)	275 mg q8h

Table 8.8   Routes of Administration of Opioids

Oral
Transdermal
Nasal
Rectal
Subcutaneous
Intramuscular
Intravenous
Epidural
Intrathecal

Opioids

Opioids are the major class of analgesics used in the management of moderate to severe cancer pain. They can be used alone or in combination with other drugs. There are various routes of administration of opioids (Table 8.8). Opioid tolerance and physical dependence are expected with long-term opioid treatment. Opioid use is also associated with side effects that should be monitored and treated accordingly.

PCA

PCA has been used for control of cancer pain. All but intramuscular routes of administration can be used for PCA. The use of PCA was first applied to cancer pain in the 1970s [9]. Oral PCA with opioids has been used with success (predetermined medication for oral use is kept at the patient's bedside) [10]. Major disadvantages of oral PCA include the risk of accidental or intentional overdose, diversion of drug to other people, and accidental ingestion by others [10, 11].

Intravenous PCA

IV PCA is the conventional method for pain control. During the patient's hospital stay, IV PCA data can be evaluated and used for calculation and conversion to oral narcotics [12]. IV PCA can also be used in an outpatient setting in which oral analgesia can no longer be administered [13, 14]. The use of IV PCA has been shown to decrease anxiety, sedation, and dependence on health care providers [13], which improves the quality of life and increases the patient's mobility. Patients on IV PCA can be trained to give anticipatory bolus doses before the onset of pain (e.g., before taking a shower). A lockout period of 30–60 minutes, with an IV PCA dose set at 50–100% of the hourly infusion rates is recommended to prevent overdosing and interference with daily activities [13]. The main indication for IV PCA is breakthrough pain with another pain control method. Compared to continuous analgesia, IV PCA has been shown to be preferred by patients [15]. IV PCA is a quick and efficient tool to determine the consistency of the analgesic response, which can guide the physician in achieving good analgesia [16]. Chronic pain is characterized by fluctuating analgesic needs. Continuous drug-delivery modes may give medication when it is not needed. Tolerance may also develop earlier than with PCA with continuous delivery systems [17].

Table 8.9   Commonly Used Agents for Epidural PCA

Preservative-free morphine sulfate
Hydromorphone
Meperidine
Bupivacaine and epinephrine
Bupivacaine and fentanyl
Bupivacaine and sufentanil
Lidocaine and fentanyl
Lidocaine and sufentanil

Patient-Controlled Epidural Analgesia

Patient-controlled epidural analgesia (PCEA) has also been offered
to cancer pain patients. PCEA is superior to continuous epidural
analgesia because of increased efficiency, higher patient satisfaction,
decreased sedation, and decreased amount of opioid used [18, 19].
Most of the work on PCEA has been carried out with patients in
acute postoperative periods and during labor analgesia. A permanent
silicone rubber epidural catheter with a subcutaneous injection post
for PCEA can be implanted in patients with chronic cancer pain.
Advantages include decreased risk of dislodgment of catheter and
epidural or site infection. Patients usually receive a loading dose with
2–3 mg of preservative-free morphine. A basal infusion of 0.4 mg per
hour can be started. PCEA dosages range from 0.5–1.0 mg per hour
(approximately 0.2 mg every 15 minutes) [17, 18]. The longer latency
of the epidural effect of morphine can be overcome with a suitable
loading dose or the addition of local anesthetics. Agents that can be
used for PCEA are listed in Table 8.9.
  PCEA is a relatively new technique and may offer adequate analgesia requiring a lower amount of total opioid usage with lower incidence of side effects. A detailed treatment plan for a patient with
chronic pain is outlined in Table 8.5.

Overall, PCA and PCEA have been found to be safe and effective means of relieving chronic pain. They can be used in hospitals to find an adequate oral dose of opioids and can be given at home by a home health care provider to improve the quality of life of a patient with cancer pain. PCEA can also be used with implanted epidural catheters.

REFERENCES

1. Bonica JJ. Treatment of Cancer Pain: Current Status and Future Needs. In HL Fields (ed), Advances in Pain Research and Therapy. New York: Raven, 1985;588.
2. Twycross RG. The relief of pain in far-advanced cancer. Reg Anesth 1980;5:2.
3. Curtis EB, Kretch R, Walsh TD. Common symptoms in patients with advanced cancer. J Palliat Care 1991;7:25.
4. Coderre JT, Katz J, Vaccariono LA, et al. Contribution of central neuroplasticity to pathological pain: review of clinical and experimental evidence. Pain 1993;52:258.
5. Asbury AK, Fields HL. Pain due to peripheral nerve damage: an hypothesis. Neurology (Cleveland) 1984;34:1587.
6. Arner S, Meyerson BA. Lack of analgesic effect of opioids on neuropathic and idiopathic forms of pain. Pain 1988;33:11.
7. Houde RW, Wallenstain SL, Beaver WT. Evaluation of Analgesics in Patients with Cancer Pain. In L Lasagna (ed), International Encyclopedia of Pharmacology and Therapeutics. Clinical Pharmacology. New York: Pergamon, 1966;58.
8. Fishman B, Pasternak S, Wallenstein SL, et al. The Memorial Pain Assessment Card: a valid instrument for the assessment of cancer pain. Cancer 1986;60:1151.
9. Keeri-Szanto M, Heaman S. Demand analgesia for relief of pain problems in terminal illness. Anesth Rev 1976;3:18.
10. Litman RS, Shapiro BS. Oral patient-controlled analgesia in adolescents. J Pain Symptom Manage 1992;7:78.
11. Coyle N. Analgesics at the bedside. Am J Nurs 1979;79:1554.
12. Baumann TJ, Batenhorst RL, Graves DA, et al. Patient-controlled analgesia in the terminally ill cancer patient. DICP Ann Pharmacother 1986;20:297.

13. Kerr IG, Sone M, DeAngelis C, et al. Continuous narcotic infusion with patient-controlled analgesia for chronic cancer pain in outpatients. Ann Intern Med 1986;108:554.

14. Swanson G, Smith J, Bulich R, et al. Patient-controlled analgesia for chronic cancer pain in the ambulatory setting: a report of 117 patients. J Clin Oncol 1989;7:1903.

15. Bruera E, Brenneis C, Michaud M, et al. Patient-controlled subcutaneous hydromorphone versus continuous subcutaneous infusion for the treatment of cancer pain. J Natl Cancer Inst 1988;80:1152.

16. Jadad AR, Carroll D, Glynn CJ, et al. Morphine responsiveness of chronic pain: double-blind randomised crossover study with patient-controlled analgesia. Lancet 1992;339:1367.

17. Marshall H, Porteous C, McMillan I, et al. Relief of pain by infusion of morphine after operation. Does tolerance develop? BMJ 1985;291:18.

18. Marlowe S, Engstrom R, White PF. Epidural patient-controlled analgesia (PCA): an alternative to continuous epidural infusions. Pain 1989;37:97.

19. Rauck R, Knarr D, Denson D, et al. Comparison of the efficacy of epidural morphine given by intermittent injection or continuous infusion for the management of postoperative pain. Anesthesiology 1986;65:A201.

9

Practical Administration of Patient-Controlled Analgesia

DEFINITION OF PCA MODES AND DOSING PARAMETERS

- *Demand dose.* A predetermined fixed dose of a drug that is self-administered by the patient pressing a button on the PCA device.
- *Lockout interval.* The time interval between patient demands during which the infuser will not administer the analgesic. It is a safety feature on PCA devices that prevents overdose.
- *One- and 4-hour limits.* An additional safety feature to prevent overdose and control cumulative dosing. The use of these limits is controversial and has both proponents and opponents.
- *Constant-rate infusion.* A fixed background of infusion of a drug is maintained. This is not truly patient controlled and should be considered to follow infusion kinetics.
- *Constant-rate infusion plus demand dosing.* A fixed background infusion supplemented by patient demand. When using a background infusion, it is important to maintain the infusion rate at a minimum to avoid ablating the necessity of patient demand.
- *Infusion demand* (not available on all models). Demands are granted as an infusion.
- *Variable-rate infusion plus demand* (not available on all models). A microprocessor monitors demand and adjusts the continuous background infusion accordingly.

Table 9.1   Guidelines for Bolus Doses and Lockout Intervals for Some Parenteral Analgesics

Drug	Bolus Dose (mg)	Lockout Interval (mins)
Agonists		
Morphine	0.5–3.0	5–20
Methadone	0.5–3.0	10–20
Hydromorphone	0.1–0.6	5–15
Oxymorphone	0.1–0.6	5–15
Meperidine	5–30	5–15
Fentanyl	0.02–0.10	3–10
Sufentanil	0.002–0.015	3–10
Agonist-antagonists		
Pentazocine	5–30	5–15
Nalbuphine	1–5	5–15
Buprenorphine	0.03–0.2	10–20

SELECTION OF A DRUG FOR PCA

In theory, any opioid can be administered by PCA. Table 9.1 lists some of the commonly used drugs.

Morphine and meperidine have been used most extensively. Hydromorphone is a good alternative. See Table 9.2 for recommended doses. Methadone and buprenorphine may be too long acting; fentanyl and its analogues are too short acting when administered as incremental bolus doses. The agonist-antagonists (e.g., nalbuphine, butorphanol) produce ceiling or plateau effects with respect to analgesia. Guidelines for dosing of opioids via PCA systems are lacking. Presently, the orders written are largely empiric.

Predictors of Opioid Dose

The best clinical predictor of opioid dose is the patient's age rather than body weight [1]. The opioid dose required for pain relief changes with patient's age due to age-related alterations in the dis-

Table 9.2   Recommended Doses for Adolescent and Adult Patients of Average Body Weight

	Loading Dose (mg)	Basal Infusion (mg/hr)	Intermittent (Hourly) Bolus Dose (mg)
Morphine	5–10	2	2
Meperidine	50–100	20	10
Hydromorphone	1.5–3.0	0.5	0.2

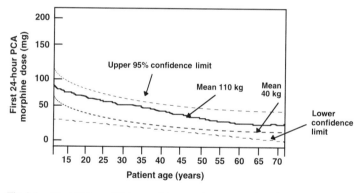

Fig. 9.1   First 24-hour PCA morphine requirements and patient age.

tribution of the drugs to different tissues, as well as changes in metabolism and excretion. There may also be age-related changes in opioid receptor numbers or binding affinities.

The weight of the patient has some effect on dose, but it is clinically insignificant compared to overall interpatient variation (Figure 9.1).

Extrapolation from the PCA morphine requirements of 1,010 opioid-naive patients in the first 24 hours after major surgery shows that after age 20 years, the first 24-hour morphine requirements decrease about 1 mg for each additional year of age, or average first 24-hour morphine requirements (mg) for patients over 20 years = 100 – (age in years) [1].

There may be an eightfold variation in dose in each age group [2]. For example, for a 60-year-old patient after major surgery, the average first 24-hour morphine requirement can be predicted to be 40 mg (i.e., 100 – 60 = 40).

MANAGEMENT OF INADEQUATE ANALGESIA

Occasionally, despite an apparently adequate setup, the patient continues to complain of pain. The physician should consider and rule out other postoperative causes (e.g., postoperative surgical complication or new injury). If the patient is receiving less than two bolus doses per hour (average), he or she should be encouraged to use the demand button more frequently. If the patient is receiving more than three bolus doses per hour (average), the size of the bolus dose should be increased by 25–50% until an effective bolus dose is determined. If the pain score is high after an additional hour, the lockout interval should be decreased by 25%.

For breakthrough pain or "reloading," twice the demand dose should be given every 5 minutes for up to five doses. During the night (sleeping) hours, the size of the demand dose should be increased or background infusion begun. The patient should be encouraged and educated to use the demand dose prophylactically before a pain-provoking event.

POSTOPERATIVE PAIN MANAGEMENT

A scheme for postoperative pain management is as follows:

Begin PCA in the postanesthesia care unit (PACU)
Loading dose: Administer twice demand dose every 5 minutes up to maximum of five doses. Make sure the patient is comfortable.

Demand dose:
    Morphine   0.5–3.0 mg
    Meperidine   5–10 mg
    Hydromorphone 0.1–0.3 mg
Lockout interval: 8 minutes
Four-hour limit:
    Morphine   30 mg
    Meperidine   300 mg
    Hydromorphone 6 mg
Optional infusion mode: Use continuously or preferably only at
    nighttime to maximize time interval between successive doses
    Morphine   0.5 mg/hr
    Meperidine   5 mg/hr
    Hydromorphone 0.1 mg/hr

Monitoring guidelines have already been described in Chapter 5.

SPECIFIC PCA APPLICATIONS

Sickle Cell Crisis

The pain of vaso-occlusive crises is usually a recurrent problem that affects adolescent patients. Besides antibiotics, hydration, and oxygen, patients require parenteral analgesics—mainly opioids. Analgesia is traditionally administered via IM injection every 3 hours.

    PCA is a useful mode of opioid administration in this setting. Some of the advantages are as follows:

1. Interruption of the pain cycle by the patient, thereby creating a feeling of control and decreasing anxiety (Figure 9.2)
2. Avoidance of erratic and variable opioid absorption from muscles (Figure 9.3)
3. Avoidance of wide swings in opioid plasma concentration
4. "Self-titration" of opioid plasma levels to the patient's own minimal effective plasma concentration

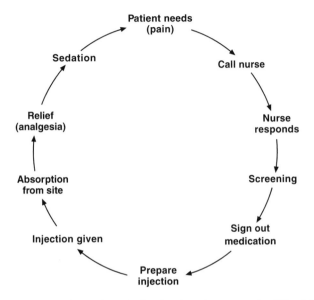

Fig. 9.2   The patient pain cycle showing the pain pattern when IM opioids are administered.

5. A combination of continuous infusion and demand dosing for 24-hour coverage of analgesia
6. Avoidance of continuous catheter techniques and therefore the need for intensive monitoring

Both meperidine and morphine [3] have been used via PCA systems for the management of pain in sickle cell crisis. Meperidine is chosen more often for the sickle cell patient, probably because of its euphoric effect. Suggested regimen with meperidine is as follows:

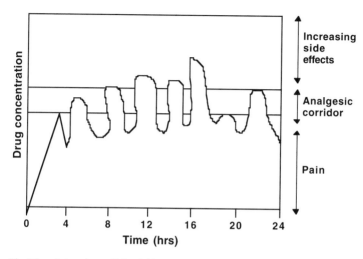

Fig. 9.3   Intermittent IM opioid analgesia.

Loading dose: 0.5 mg/kg
Demand dose: 0.2 mg/kg
Lockout interval: 15 minutes

   An alternative approach to severe pain in sickle cell crisis is to use a combination of a loading dose, basal infusion, and intermittent bolus doses. Therapy should be combined with oxygen, hydration, and antibiotics to cover infections and down titration of opioid dosages. Adjuvant therapy includes use of anxiolytics, epidural dilute local anesthetic infusions, hypnosis, biofeedback, heating pads, and in some cases, blood transfusion.

In sickle cell crisis pain, initially modest parenteral opioid dosages should be used for effective analgesia. Down titration with time avoids untoward effects. Patients who use PCA usually stop using the machine spontaneously in 3–4 days, as pain intensity decreases. In other cases, IV forms can be converted to equianalgesic oral opioid forms or even milder analgesics or nonsteroidal analgesics.

Angina Pectoris

Patients may experience anginal pain even after optimal medical treatment or revascularization. Traditional opioid administration may cause intermittent pain relief and unacceptable side effects.

In one study, a thoracic epidural catheter was implanted subcutaneously followed by self-administration of opioids. Patient-controlled epidural analgesia (PCEA) with demand doses of 2–3 mg three times per day was used. Pain relief occurred in all patients with resumption of physical activity in some cases [4]. While further research is necessary, PCEA appears to hold promise as an effective long-term therapy for persistent angina pectoris after coronary revascularization.

Treatment of Cancer Pain

The following factors intrinsic to oncologic pain complicate its effective treatment: (1) Neuropathic pain in cancer is often resistant to opioids; (2) oncologic pain is multifocal (e.g., visceral pain, bone pain, metastatic pain); (3) chronic cancer pain may be superimposed on acute exacerbations (i.e., infection, spread of cancer, new tumor); (4) pain perception is intertwined with the emotional state of the patient.

PCA is principally indicated for mentally competent patients whose pain is not relieved by oral medications or who cannot tolerate oral or enteral opioids because of gastrointestinal disturbances. PCA is also particularly useful in the treatment of breakthrough pain. Based on studies to date, PCA can be safely and effectively administered subcutaneously or via IV in the inpatient or outpatient setting (see Chapter 8). To optimize therapy, treatment should be started in the hospital so that assessments of response and toxicity can be made.

If the analgesic requirements of the patient are unknown, the suggested regimen [5] is as follows:

1. Morphine, 2 mg every 15 minutes until pain relief is achieved. Loading should occur over 4 hours to evaluate the patient's needs.
2. After 4 hours, the total dose of morphine should be divided by the number of hours spent in loading (e.g., 20 mg morphine in 4 hours = 5 mg morphine/hour).
3. Over the next 4 hours, 60% of the hourly dose becomes the demand dose with a lockout interval of 10 minutes (i.e., 60% of 5 mg = 3 mg demand dose via PCA with a lockout of 10 minutes). The final titration of the patient's analgesic requirement is thus known.
4. A demand dose that is equivalent to the amount of opioid used over a preceding 90-minute period is then selected. A 15-minute lockout interval is given (e.g., if the patient self-administered eight 3-mg doses over 240 minutes, a 9-mg demand dose is given with a lockout interval of 15 minutes).

Patients with cancer generally tolerate large demand doses, as the intensity of their pain is great. Monitoring follows the respiratory rate and mental status. A decrease in respiratory rate of 40% or more with hypoxemia or somnolence indicates the need for closer observation and adjustment of the dosing parameters [6].

Two major concerns are overdosage and opioid abuse [7]. Proper infuser settings can minimize these risks and most studies suggest a very low risk of opioid abuse.

PCA in Children and Adolescents

PCA with opioids is an attractive alternative to the conventional IM administration of opioids for the management of postoperative pain in children requiring extensive, extended, or recurrent opioid analgesia [8].

The major advantage of PCA in children and adolescents is the patient's ability to control his or her own pain treatment without relying on nursing personnel. Its major disadvantage is that patient mobility can be restricted and it does require maintenance of an IV line.

Children 8 years of age or older who can understand how to operate the PCA infuser and recognize different intensities of pain are suitable candidates for PCA. A good screening test to use is to ask children to rate three common painful experiences using a 0- to 10- scale, for example a bee sting, a mosquito bite, and skinned shins and hands from a bicycle accident. If they rate all three experiences at the same intensity or only as either zero or 10, they are judged to be inappropriate candidates for PCA and a conventional treatment modality is used. Otherwise, a trial of PCA can be used [9].

Children 5–7 years of age are also eligible for PCA but may require either parental or nursing assistance (see Chapter 4).

Recommendations for initiating PCA therapy in children are as follows:

Discontinue all other pain orders
Use (only) morphine 1 mg/ml via PCA pump (meperidine or fentanyl can be substituted)
Initiate PCA in the PACU
    Loading dose: 0.05 mg/kg in divided doses
    Demand dose: 0.02 mg/kg
    Lockout interval: 15 minutes
    Background infusion: optional

PCA opioid doses may be adjusted in the following circumstances:

1. Pain intensity ratings of six or more with minimal sedation are registered. Therapy is achieved by (a) decreasing the lockout interval to 10 minutes, (b) adding background infusion of 25% of the daytime hourly morphine requirement (e.g., if a 5-year-old who weighs 20 kg is using 1.6 mg of morphine per hour, a background

infusion of 0.4 mg morphine per hour should be used without making any changes to the demand dose or lockout interval).

2. Pain scores are less than 2 and the child is asleep most of the time. The demand dose or background infusion should be reduced.

Data Collection

Children and their parents should be familiarized with the PCA systems and data collection systems (Figure 9.4) before surgery. This education greatly enhances the success of PCA therapy. Children older than 7 years can use the linear analogue pain scale (Figure 9.5). Parents of patients under 7 years of age can use the analogue scale to rate their child's pain. Additional input is given by the nursing service using the objective pain discomfort scale (Table 9.3). The sedation scale also provides useful data:

1. Awake, alert
2. Awake, drowsy
3. Asleep

Labor Pain

Labor is a complex pain model. The intensity of labor pain compared with other painful conditions is depicted in Figure 9.6. Several options for labor analgesia exist. PCA with IV opioids during labor is a new and underused modality. Although epidural analgesia with local anesthetic plus opioids is the gold standard, PCA can be offered to those who do not want epidural analgesia or at institutions in which an epidural service is not available. Clearly, PCA offers several advantages over intermittent dosing with opioids. Placing the parturient in charge of her analgesia and freeing nursing time are logistic benefits. A small dose of opioids given more frequently is preferable to a larger dose administered less often. If delivery occurs in the hour or two after injection of a small dose, the infant is less likely to be depressed by the medication.

Time	Date	Linear Analogue Scale	Sedation Score	Pain Discomfort Score	PCA Morphine (mg/hr)

Morphine use per shift:

Tour 1: _____ mg; Tour 2: _____ mg; Tour 3: _____ mg

Fig. 9.4   Sample data collection systems.

Meperidine has been the most widely used opioid for labor analgesia. Suggested dosages for IV PCA using meperidine and nalbuphine are as follows:

For meperidine
    Loading dose: none
    Demand dose: 15 mg
    Lockout interval: 10 minutes
For nalbuphine
    Loading dose: none

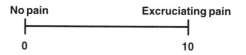

Fig. 9.5   Linear analogue pain scale.

Table 9.3   Objective Pain Discomfort Scale

	Observation	Criteria	Points
A	Blood pressure	±10% preoperative	0
		9–20% preoperative	1
		>20% preoperative	2
B	Crying	Not crying	0
		Crying but responds to tender loving care (TLC)	1
		Crying and does not respond to TLC	2
C	Moving	None	0
		Restlessness	1
		Thrashing	2
D	Agitation	Patient asleep or calm	0
		Mild	1
		Hysterical	2
E	Body language	Patient asleep	0
		Mild pain (cannot localize)	1
		Moderate pain (can localize verbally or by pointing)	2

Demand dose: 3 mg
Lockout interval: 10 minutes

Postcesarean Pain

Pain management following cesarean delivery offers a unique challenge. Improved analgesic therapy is unlikely to improve the low morbidity and mortality inherent in this healthy group of patients.

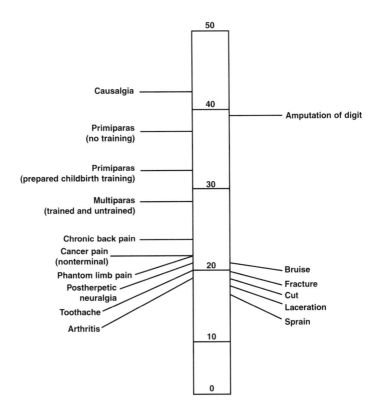

Fig. 9.6   Pain (relative intensity) scores.

Table 9.4   Advantages of IV PCA in Obstetrics Over Conventional Analgesic Techniques

Greater patient satisfaction
Same or better analgesia
Decreased drug usage
Decreased demands on nursing staff
Comparable in cost (once PCA services are established)
Equally safe
Decreased side effects

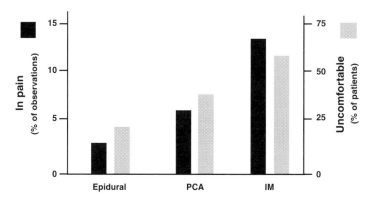

Fig. 9.7   Comparison of IV PCA versus epidural morphine and IM morphine.

Nevertheless, most women desire to be awake and interact with their newborn, family, and visitors. These needs are poorly met by standard IM opioid regimens. IV PCA and epidural opioids appear to be superior and viable options.

IV PCA has a number of merits compared to IM opioids (Table 9.4).

As-needed IM opioids have been compared to IV PCA morphine and epidural morphine in at least two studies (Figure 9.7). Epidural morphine provided the best analgesia in these studies [10, 11]. The two shortcomings of morphine were that analgesia for the entire 24-hour period was not adequate for all patients, and several patients had bothersome side effects.

Recommendations

1.   If the patient elects epidural anesthesia for cesarean delivery, one dose of lipid-soluble opioid (e.g., fentanyl) may be administered at the institution of the block or immediately after the birth of the baby. An additional dose may be given on admission to the recovery room, and a PCA infuser system with an opioid (e.g., morphine or meperidine) is initiated.

2.   If the patient elects spinal anesthesia for cesarean delivery, one dose of lipid-soluble opioid (e.g., fentanyl) is administered at the institution of the block, which provides 2–6 hours of analgesia. On admission to the recovery room, a PCA infuser is initiated.

3.   For cesarean section under general anesthesia, the PCA infuser can be initiated in the PACU similar to any other case (see earlier section on Postoperative Pain Management).

4.   In obstetrics, meperidine (Demerol) has been used more commonly, although morphine can be substituted. The dose regimen is similar to that discussed previously. A background infusion mode is seldom required.

ALTERNATIVE ROUTES FOR PCA

PCA provides improved titration of analgesic medication, thereby minimizing individual pharmacokinetic and pharmacodynamic differences. Recent studies suggest that PCA can be highly effective when administered by a variety of alternative routes, such as

1.   Sublingual
2.   Transmucosal
3.   Subcutaneous
4.   Epidural

For more extensive operative procedures, PCEA may offer significant advantages with respect to the ability to improve analgesia and enhance recovery of bodily functions. PCEA combines the inherent analgesic effectiveness of the epidural route of administration with the flexibility in dosage titration offered by PCA. Additionally, PCEA uses less total opioid compared with continuous infusion and as-needed IM opioid injections.

Tables 9.5 and 9.6 outline dosing guidelines for PCEA. Table 9.7 outlines recommendations for fixed-interval IM opioids. Table 9.8 outlines recommendations for opioid administration via subcutaneous PCA.

Table 9.5   Dosing Guidelines for Epidural Opioid Analgesia

Opioid	Site of Administration	Intermittent Bolus Technique*	Continuous Infusion Technique	Adjunctive Therapy
Morphine	Lumbar catheters for incisions below T8; thoracic catheters for upper abdominal and thoracic surgery	Administer a 3- to 8-mg bolus in 10 ml preservative-free saline q8–24h as clinically indicated	2- to 4-mg bolus followed by infusion (50 µg/ml) at 8–15 ml/hr via lumbar catheters; 4–8 ml/hr thoracic catheters	IV ketorolac 15–30 mg q6h; epidural bupivacaine 0.03–0.10%
Hydromorphone	Lumbar catheters for incisions below T8; thoracic catheters for upper abdominal and thoracic surgery	0.5- to 1.5-mg bolus q5–10h	0.5- to 1.5-mg bolus followed by infusion (10 µg/ml) at 8–15 ml/hr via lumbar catheters; 4–8 ml/hr thoracic catheters	IV ketorolac 15–30 mg q6h; epidural bupivacaine 0.03–0.10%
Meperidine	Lumbar catheters for incisions below T10; thoracic catheters for upper abdominal and thoracic surgery	50- to 75-mg bolus q4–8h	50- to 75-mg bolus followed by infusion (100 µg/ml) at 8–15 ml/hr via lumbar catheters; 4–8 ml/hr thoracic catheters	IV ketorolac 15–30 mg q6h; epidural bupivacaine 0.03–0.10%

Fentanyl	Lumbar catheters for incisions below T12; thoracic catheters for all other incisions	50- to 100-µg bolus q2–3h (not recommended)	50- to 100-µg bolus followed by infusion (5 µg/ml) at 8–15 ml/hr via lumbar catheter; 4–8 ml/hr thoracic catheter	IV/IM ketorolac 15–30 mg q6h; epidural bupivacaine 0.05–0.10%
Sufentanil	Lumbar catheters for incision below T12; thoracic catheters for all other incisions	20- to 30-µg bolus every 2–3 hrs (not recommended)	20- to 30-µg bolus followed by infusion (1–2 µg/ml) at 8–15 lumbar catheters; 4–8 ml/hr thoracic catheters	IV/IM ketorolac 15–30 mg q6h; epidural bupivacaine 0.05–0.10% or less

*Dependent on age, physical status, height, extent of surgical dissection, etc.
T8 = eighth thoracic vertebra; T10 = tenth thoracic vertebra; T12 = twelfth thoracic vertebra.

Table 9.6   Epidural PCA Dosing Guidelines

Opioid	Concentration (µg/ml)	Loading Dose*	Epidural PCA Dose* (ml)	Lockout (mins)	Continuous Rate*	4-Hr Limit (ml)
Morphine	50	2–4 mg	2–4	9–15	6–12 ml/hr	40–70
Hydromorphone	10	500–1,500 µg	2–4	6–10	6–12 ml/hr	40–70
Fentanyl	5	75–100 µg	2–4	6	6–15 ml/hr	40–70
Sufentanil	2	0.5 µg/kg	2–4	6	0.1 µg/hr	40–70

*Dependent on site of epidural catheter, extent of surgery, and patient's physical status.

Table 9.7   Titration of Intermittent Intravenous/ Subcutaneous Opioids

Requirements

Initial age-related range of morphine doses based on average daily requirements	Approximate average 24-hour morphine requirement for patients older than 20 years = (100 – age)
	Single dose = average 24-hour morphine requirement ÷ 8
Appropriate dose interval	For example, 2 hourly as needed or fixed interval
Monitoring of sedation score, pain score, and respiratory rate	For example, at time of injection and 1 hour after injection
Monitoring for other side effects	
Selection of subsequent doses according to patient response	

Aims

Patient comfort
Sedation score <2
Respiratory rate >8/min

Table 9.8   Guidelines for Opioid Administration via Subcutaneous PCA*

Drug (concentration)	Demand Dose	Lockout Interval (mins)
Morphine (50 mg/ml)	0.2 ml = 1 mg	10
Hydromorphone (1.0 mg/ml)	0.2 ml = 0.2 mg	15
Oxymorphone (1.5 mg/ml)	0.2 ml = 0.3 mg	10

*Compared to IV PCA, more concentrated solutions and smaller dose volumes are used to minimize the fluid volume administered.

REFERENCES

1. Macintyre PE, Jarvis DA. Age is the best predictor of postoperative morphine requirements. Pain 1996;64:357.
2. Austin KL, Stapleton JV, Malher LE. Relationship between blood meperidine concentration and analgesic response to meperidine. Anesthesiology 1980;53:460.
3. Schecter NL, Barrich FB, Katz SM. The use of patient controlled analgesia in adolescents with sickle cell pain crisis: a preliminary report. J Pain Symptom Manage 1988;3:109.
4. Clemenson SE, Thayssen P, Hole P. Epidural morphine for out patients with severe anginal pain. BMJ 1987;294:475.
5. Citron ML, Johnston-Early A, Boyer M, et al. Patient controlled analgesia for severe cancer pain. Arch Intern Med 1986;146:734.
6. Citron ML, Johnston-Early A, Fossieck B, et al. Safety and efficacy of continuous intravenous morphine for severe cancer pain. Am J Med 1984;77:199.
7. Kanner RB, Foley KM. Use and abuse of narcotic analgesics in a cancer pain clinic [abstract]. Proc Am Assoc Cancer Res 1980;21:381.
8. Brown RE, Broadman LM. Patient controlled analgesia (PCA) for postoperative pain control in adolescents [abstract]. Anesth Analg 1987;66:S22
9. Broadman LM, Brown RE, Rice LJ, et al. Patient controlled analgesia in children and adolescents: a report of postoperative pain management in 150 patients [abstract]. Anesth Analg 1989;71:A11.

10. Esenach JC, Ance SC, Dewan DM. Patient controlled analgesia following cesarean section: a comparison with epidural and intravenous narcotics. Anesth Analg 1988;68:444.
11. Harrison DM, Sinatra RM, Morgese L, et al. Epidural narcotic and patient-controlled analgesia for post-cesarean section pain relief. Anesthesiology 1988;68:454.

10

Patient-Controlled Analgesia: Administrative and Economic Issues

PCA is a viable therapeutic alternative to the conventional intramuscular administration of opioids. Some of the advantages are listed in Table 10.1. Some possible drawbacks also exist (Table 10.2). In establishing and managing an efficient PCA service, several issues must be addressed (Table 10.3).

COMPONENTS OF A PCA SERVICE

1. Anesthesiologists are well suited to work in an acute pain service because of their knowledge of the neurophysiology of pain transmission and experience with opioids and local anesthetics. Anesthesia personnel must be available at all times.
2. Nurse practitioners are best suited for collecting patient information, selecting patients for PCA, and above all, educating patients.

Ideally, the best time to introduce the concept of PCA is during the preoperative anesthesia assessment clinic, reinforcing it again on the morning before the scheduled surgery. Nurses can also assist during rounds and patient follow ups and by maintaining records. Nursing staff should develop policies and procedures that address the issues listed in Table 10.4.

Table 10.1   Merits of PCA Systems

Pain management is improved
Pain control increases
Nursing time is decreased
Total amount of opioid used by the patient may be decreased
Drug use is more effective
Control is placed in the hands of the patient, who can titrate his or her
     own therapy, increasing patient independence and decreasing reliance
     on others
Patients are generally more satisfied and leave with a better perception
     of their hospital experience

Table 10.2   Drawbacks of PCA Systems

New machinery must be bought, learned, and maintained
New protocols need to be designed (administrative and clinical)
Continuous IV infusion of maintenance fluid must be maintained
Side effects of drugs (e.g., itching, nausea, and pump malfunction) must
     be attended to promptly

Table 10.3   Organization of a PCA Service

Establish an organization, a pain-management service, consisting of a
     nurse practitioner, pharmacist, anesthesiologist, and secretarial support
     for billing.
Train all nursing personnel who will be involved in the care of the post-
     operative pain patient.
Advertise pain-management service throughout the hospital and com-
     munity through seminars, staff meetings, and clinical conferences.
Prepare a policies manual that explains patient selection and education
     and PCA initiation, maintenance, and termination.
Streamline procedures that allow for simple writing of orders, efficient
     patient rounds, and contingency plans for inadequate analgesia and
     complications.

Table 10.4   Nursing Roles in Acute Pain Service and PCA Service

Setup and operation of PCA service
Recommendation of patient control mode (demand dosing, continuous
    infusion plus demand dosing)
Injector cartridge availability and storage
Interruption of infusion
Discontinuation of infusion
Response to alarm systems
Troubleshooting procedures
Documentation requirements
Monitoring requirements
Liaison with pain service and control pharmacy

The pharmacist has an important role in the pain-management team for the following reasons:

1. The pharmacist is the most experienced and reliable controller of PCA drugs, especially in view of the record maintenance that the program requires.
2. The pharmacist is best positioned to coordinate the prescribing, dispensing, and administration of opioids and integrate the PCA program into existing systems.
3. The pharmacist can develop an efficient and effective program that balances the concerns and preferences of physicians, pharmacists, nurses, and patients.
4. The pharmacist is experienced in dealing with most PCA vendors and knows their reliability, market orientation, and service record. The pharmacist also knows how to request competitive bids and evaluate lease/buy options.
5. The pharmacist can perform objective cost/benefit analyses, including labor and supply costs of alternative drug distribution systems.

Table 10.5   Pharmacist's Role in Acute Pain Service/PCA Service

Role in conjunction with other members of the PCA implementation
    team:
    Writes PCA protocol
    Defines patient population
    Develops cost versus benefit analysis
Describes and implements opioid control and distribution plan
Describes and implements device protocol
Provides in-service education to patients, nurses, and physicians
Develops prescription form
Develops drug compatibility form
Develops drug, adverse reactions, and patient monitoring forms
Monitors all PCA patients daily and screens for
    Analgesic efficacy
    Toxicity
    Device malfunction
Maintains communication with nurses and physicians
Member of PCA quality assurance committee

Based on his experience as described above, the role of the pharmacist in the PCA service is outlined in Table 10.5. Figure 10.1 shows a
model setup for an acute pain service.

OTHER ADMINISTRATIVE CONSIDERATIONS

Suggested guidelines for starting PCA in postoperative patients are
as follows:

1. A patient is evaluated by the PCA team only after consultation
    with the primary physician.
2. Discuss the PCA scheme with the patient preoperatively and with
    the surgeon intraoperatively.
3. Ideally, PCA should be initiated with the desired settings in the
    postanesthesia care unit (PACU).
4. All information and forms needed for the daily operation should
    be stored in the PACU (e.g., preprinted order forms, patient data
    sheets, policies, procedures, log book, record book).

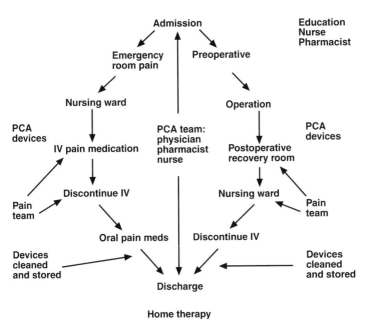

Fig. 10.1 The PCA team.

5. Maintain a log book that serves as a permanent record of the PCA service and a backup for the daily visits book.
6. A daily visits book should be carried to the wards for record keeping and updating patient data forms.

ECONOMIC ISSUES OF PCA

The economic impact of PCA on the health care system occurs at various points:

1. Hospital administrators are faced with requests for PCA infusers, related materials, and drugs that superficially appear expensive. The initial response is often negative.
2. Physicians must acquire new knowledge, assume new administrative and medical responsibilities, and devote additional professional time if PCA is to be used effectively and safely.
3. Health insurance carriers, both government and private, will notice new charges levied upon their clients for pain control. Maintaining that pain control is part of anesthesia care, and charges may be and often are denied.

Patient expectations also need to be considered. As the general public becomes knowledgeable about PCA as an option for pain control, consumer pressure will be brought to bear on hospitals, physicians, and health insurance providers to pay for state-of-the-art and contemporary treatment of pain.

PCA Reimbursement Issues

The Health Care Financing Administration (HCFA) has provided few rules on the subject of Medicare reimbursement for pain-management services, leaving most of the payment decisions to Medicare carriers. In addition, pain relief is highly subjective and, therefore, difficult to quantify and document. Consequently, billing and reimbursement policies vary widely across carriers. In fact, the only consistency one may find is in what Medicare does not cover. Anesthesiologists and anesthetists nationwide agree that Medicare reimbursement for pain-control services is inadequate: in some places, according to physicians, as little as 30 cents on the dollar.

Pain management is a multidisciplinary field; programs may include psychotherapy, physical therapy, exercise physiology, and biofeedback, as well as medication management. Programs typically teach people to control and live with their pain in addition to attempting to reduce pain through medications. Pain-management services can generally be divided into three categories: (1) acute pain management, (2) chronic pain management, (3) cancer pain management. This section only covers PCA that is part of acute pain management.

Billing for PCA

Medicare payment for physician services related to PCA is included in the surgeon's global fee and is never paid separately. Medicare considers other services provided by the hospital nursing staff in administering pain medications to be routine hospital expenses, and these reimbursements are included in the Medicare Part A prospective payment (diagnosis-related group) for the hospital stay.

Of note is the fact that even though HCFA has a national policy on pain-management services, it has left much of the interpretation of the policy to the local Medicare Part B carriers. Consequently what constitutes, for example, a "medically necessary" pain procedure that is worthy of separate payment (in addition to surgeon's pay) varies widely across carrier areas. For example, if an anesthesiologist initiates PCA in the recovery room only after written consultation from the surgeon, some carriers will allow PCA setup time into the anesthesia time units. After that, PCA is considered routine postoperative pain management and cannot be billed. Similarly, PCA given for nonsurgical pain control is not eligible for payment as a separate service because it is considered an integral part of a doctor's medical care. Epidural PCA, however, can be billed separately if it has been initiated solely for the purpose of analgesia and was not an integral part of the anesthetic.

SELECTED READING

1. Harmer M, Rosen M, Vickers MD. Patient Controlled Analgesia. Oxford: Blackwell, 1985.
2. Ferrante FM, Ostheimer GW, Covino BG. Patient-Controlled Analgesia. Boston: Blackwell Scientific, 1990.
3. Heath ML, Thomas VJ. Patient-Controlled Analgesia: Confidence in Postoperative Pain Control. Oxford: Oxford University Press, 1993.

Index